THE EVERYTHING®
GUIDE TO THE
LOW-FODMAP DIET

Dear Reader,

Although we come from different perspectives, we share a deep under-standing of the real hardships of living with IBS. We are so grateful a diet has been developed that quiets symptoms and turns people's lives around.

Barbara has been actively covering the low-FODMAP diet since the first research articles started coming out of Australia. Every day she hears heartbreaking stories about what it's like to live with IBS. It's been so gratifying to be able to introduce to clients and online readers a way of eating that brings true symptom relief.

Diagnosed with IBS in 2011, Kathleen has studied the FODMAP diet extensively in an effort to ease her own symptoms. She has real-life expe-rience in putting low-FODMAP recipes on the table. By sharing them with you, she hopes to provide comfort, during the Elimination Phase and beyond—in the most delicious, nutritious sense of the word!

We are thrilled at the opportunity to help ease your IBS symptoms by supporting you in following the low-FODMAP diet. We know that making dietary changes is not an easy process, but you are not alone. Through the pages of this book and via our website, *www.EverythingLowFODMAP.com*, we are here to help you every step of the way.

Dr. Barbara Bolen

Kathleen Bradley, CPC

Welcome to the EVERYTHING® Series!

These handy, accessible books give you all you need to tackle a difficult project, gain a new hobby, comprehend a fascinating topic, prepare for an exam, or even brush up on something you learned back in school but have since forgotten.

You can choose to read an Everything® book from cover to cover or just pick out the information you want from our four useful boxes: e-questions, e-facts, e-alerts, and e-ssentials.

We give you everything you need to know on the subject, but throw in a lot of fun stuff along the way, too.

We now have more than 400 Everything® books in print, spanning such wide-ranging categories as weddings, pregnancy, cooking, music instruction, foreign language, crafts, pets, New Age, and so much more. When you're done reading them all, you can finally say you know Everything®!

QUESTION

Answers to common questions

FACT

Important snippets of information

ALERT

Urgent warnings

ESSENTIAL

Quick handy tips

PUBLISHER Karen Cooper

MANAGING EDITOR, EVERYTHING® SERIES Lisa Laing

COPY CHIEF Casey Ebert

ASSISTANT PRODUCTION EDITOR Alex Guarco

ACQUISITIONS EDITOR Lisa Laing

SENIOR DEVELOPMENT EDITOR Brett Palana-Shanahan

EVERYTHING® SERIES COVER DESIGNER Erin Alexander

Visit the entire Everything® series at *www.everything.com*

THE
EVERYTHING®
GUIDE TO THE
LOW-FODMAP
DIET

A healthy plan for managing IBS
and other digestive disorders

Dr. Barbara Bolen and Kathleen Bradley, CPC

Adams Media
New York London Toronto Sydney New Delhi

Barbara would like to dedicate this book to the many courageous individuals who have shared their intimate struggles with her over so many years, as well as to her family for their support of all of her varied (to put it mildly) endeavors.

Kathleen would like to dedicate this book to all who share the burden of living with IBS; to her parents, who fostered a lifelong love of cooking and creativity; and to her husband and boys for bringing so much joy into her kitchen and life.

Adams Media
An Imprint of Simon & Schuster, Inc.
57 Littlefield Street
Avon, Massachusetts 02322

An Everything® Series Book.
Everything® and everything.com® are registered trademarks of Simon & Schuster, Inc.

ADAMS MEDIA and colophon are trademarks of Simon & Schuster, Inc.

For information about special discounts for bulk purchases, please contact Simon & Schuster Special Sales at 1-866-506-1949 or business@simonandschuster.com.

The Simon & Schuster Speakers Bureau can bring authors to your live event. For more information or to book an event contact the Simon & Schuster Speakers Bureau at 1-866-248-3049 or visit our website at www.simonspeakers.com.

Photographs by Vita Bella Photography
Nutritional statistics by Nicole Cormier, RD

Manufactured in the United States of America

8 2020

Library of Congress Cataloging-in-Publication Data has been applied for.

ISBN 978-1-4405-8173-1
ISBN 978-1-4405-8174-8 (ebook)

Contents

Acknowledgments

This book would not have been possible were it not for the hard work of the low-FODMAP diet pioneers. These include Susan J. Shepherd, PhD; Peter R. Gibson, MD; Jacqueline S. Barrett, PhD; and all of the other researchers at Monash University in Australia. It is awe-inspiring how their work is spreading worldwide. Their dedication to the diet continues with their ever-so-helpful updates regarding the FODMAP content of common foods. In the United States, pioneers Patsy Catsos, MS, RD, LD, and Kate Scarlata, RD, LDN, are to be commended for their work in providing comprehensive and up-to-date information on all aspects of the diet.

The authors would like to thank Lisa Laing, Brett Palana-Shanahan, Kate Petrella, and the Adams Media team. Our gratitude also goes to Andrea Costrino and Jessica Dolly of Vita Bella Photography for their food styling and photographic talents. A special thanks to Imran Zaffer, MD, for sharing his experience and expertise. Much appreciation for Paul Olszewski and the Patrick family, for tasting nearly every recipe in this book, and to Thomas Bolen for tasting a few. We are very thankful for health coaches Ami Patrick and Katie Hussong, along with the Institute for Integrative Nutrition's stellar health coach training program, for opening our eyes to a new way of cooking, baking, and living life. And most importantly, we are ever so grateful to Claire Bradley for her endless showering of support and love.

Introduction

IRRITABLE BOWEL SYNDROME (IBS) may just be one of the most confusing and frustrating of all human ailments. In IBS, the digestive system has gone haywire, yet doctors see nothing wrong. One person with IBS may have bouts of urgent diarrhea, while the next deals with chronic constipation. Both may experience abdominal pain, whether it be a dull ache or cramps so severe that one is doubled over in pain. To make matters worse, doctors have had very little to offer their IBS patients in terms of bringing about symptom relief.

If you have IBS, you know firsthand how disruptive the symptoms can be. Being in physical pain, needing to be near a bathroom at all times, and worrying about what to eat can make it extremely hard to live a normal life. IBS makes it difficult to go to school, to deal with work demands, and to commit to fun activities. It can have a negative impact on relationships, family life, and one's social life. Travel can be cause for great anxiety or may have to be avoided at all costs.

To feel so sick and to be told by doctors that not only is there nothing wrong, but also that not much can be done about it, can be devastating. The hunt for relief can be maddening—either nothing works or what seemed to be working suddenly stops working. Trying to figure out what to eat can be a nightmare. Sometimes it seems like what you eat runs right through you, or makes you more gassy and bloated, or causes your colon to rebel with painful spasms. Your doctor told you to eat more fiber, but that backfired. You are sick and tired of dealing with your body and you are struggling to maintain hope that things can get better.

You can be greatly encouraged to hear that there is a new treatment in town—a treatment that has research backing its effectiveness in getting rid of those awful IBS symptoms. This means no more pain, no more gas and bloating, and what is sure to be an extremely welcomed return to regular bowel movements. This revolutionary treatment is the low-FODMAP diet.

The low-FODMAP diet has been designed, tested, and refined by researchers from Monash University in Australia. The work of these researchers has changed the way that IBS patients are treated in Australia, and this effect is spreading worldwide. Their work on the diet is expanding beyond IBS, as they are finding that the diet may be helpful for anyone who experiences chronic intestinal problems. You can reap the benefits of this diet simply by learning about it and then putting it into practice.

FODMAP is an acronym used to describe certain carbohydrates found in common foods that contribute to unwanted digestive symptoms due to the way they act within the digestive system. At its simplest, the diet involves avoiding foods high in FODMAPs and eating those that are low in FODMAPs. Best results are achieved if you completely restrict high-FODMAP foods from your diet for a short period of time and then slowly reintroduce them to see how your body reacts.

This book will take the mystery out of the term FODMAP and guide you step-by-step through the process of following the diet. You will be given several options, whether that be a full FODMAP elimination or a more casual approach. Along the way you will learn more about how your digestive system works and what is going wrong when a person has IBS. If you are not so interested in the science, you can feel free to move right into learning about what you can now do to make yourself feel better (see Chapter 3). You will find tips for shopping, dining out, and socializing. Strategies are also included for supporting children on the diet and managing the diet if you are a vegetarian.

Following a low-FODMAP diet means that you are no longer stuck with eating bland, boring food. As you identify which foods you need to stay clear of, you will find yourself free to eat a wide variety of food with confidence. In this book, you will find inventive, delicious recipes, all made with low-FODMAP ingredients, that you can enjoy from day one of the diet. Each recipe includes wholesome ingredients to help ensure that your nutrition needs are being met so that you can experience optimal overall health alongside your newly found digestive health.

CHAPTER 1

What Is the Low-FODMAP Diet?

The low-FODMAP diet was designed to help you get rid of those IBS symptoms of abdominal pain, bloating, constipation, diarrhea, and flatulence that you know so well. The diet is based on scientifically backed knowledge regarding food components known collectively as FODMAPs. In the beginning of the diet you will avoid all foods that are high in FODMAPs, and then you will systematically identify which specific types of FODMAPs are causing your problems. The goal of the diet is to get you to a place where you can eat a wide range of foods without experiencing symptoms.

The Science Behind the Diet

The low-FODMAP diet was developed by researchers at Monash University in Australia. Through their work, they were able to identify certain food components that they believed contributed to digestive symptoms in patients with IBS. These food components consist of short-chain carbohydrates (saccharides) and sugar alcohols (polyols). By taking the first letter from the word "fermentable" and then the first letter from each group of carbohydrates (oligosaccharides, disaccharides, monosaccharides, and polyols), they were able to coin the term "FODMAP." These researchers put people with IBS on diets that restricted them from eating foods that were high in FODMAPs and then assessed their symptoms. Overwhelmingly, they found that IBS symptoms were significantly reduced by the diet.

With refinement and further testing, these FODMAP researchers have further broken down the FODMAP classification into specific types. Subsequently, they have found that some individuals are more sensitive to certain FODMAP types than others. This finding allows the diet to be more individualized and helps to expand the range of food that people with IBS can enjoy with confidence.

ESSENTIAL

You may not be sensitive to every type of FODMAP. It is essential for your overall health that you take the time to determine which FODMAPs you are sensitive to through the Challenge Phase of the diet. Restricting only the FODMAPs that you are sensitive to allows you to eat a wider range of food and therefore a greater range of nutrients.

As part of their work, Monash University researchers have conducted laboratory analyses of a wide variety of foods in order to identify whether or not they are high in FODMAPs, as well as to identify which particular FODMAP each one contains. Their work continues today as they classify new foods according to their FODMAP content.

How Digestion Works

In order for you to best understand how a low-FODMAP diet will be of help to you, it is important that you become reacquainted with how digestion works. You were most likely taught this in high school biology, but the details may now be a distant memory!

Initial Stages of Digestion

Digestion is basically the process by which the foods that you eat are broken down so that your body can absorb their nutrients. The initial stages of digestion are quite familiar to you. Digestion begins in your mouth, both with the act of chewing and with the action of enzymes present in saliva. Food then makes its way down into your stomach, where it is further broken down by hydrochloric acid and an enzyme named pepsin.

The Small Intestine

Digestion gets a bit more complicated as food moves beyond your stomach. The contents of the stomach are emptied into the small intestine as a substance called "chyme." Your small intestine has three parts: the duodenum, the jejunum, and the ileum. In the duodenum, the chyme is mixed with pancreatic enzymes and bile, which is produced by the liver but stored in the gallbladder. Enzymes from the pancreas break down carbohydrates, fat, and protein. Bile is necessary for the breakdown of fats.

FACT

The small intestine is lined with hairlike projections called "villi." When a person with celiac disease eats gluten, the villi are damaged due to an autoimmune response. This damage results in a state in which vital nutrients are not absorbed, leading to serious health problems. Therefore, a person who has celiac disease should never eat gluten-containing foods.

In the jejunum and the ileum, the nutrients from the food that you eat are broken down and absorbed into the bloodstream. Fiber is what is left over from this process, as fiber cannot not be broken down and absorbed. The small intestine empties fiber, along with water, into the large intestine.

The Large Intestine

In your large intestine, water is absorbed, resulting in the formation of stool. The large intestine has several parts: the ascending colon, the transverse colon, the descending colon, the sigmoid colon, and the rectum. Fecal matter makes its way down through your large intestine, firming up as it travels along, in preparation to be evacuated through a bowel movement.

Your large intestine is populated by a large number of microorganisms. These microorganisms are called the "gut flora" and are predominantly made up of bacteria, but also consist of some fungi, such as yeast, and protozoa. The gut bacteria play an important role in your health, as they help to support the immune system. Illness or antibiotic use, among other things, can result in the gut bacteria being out of balance, a state called "dysbiosis."

Gut bacteria also play a role in some digestive symptoms. Food components, most notably carbohydrates (sugars) that are not absorbed by the small intestine will be set upon by the gut bacteria. The result of this interaction is fermentation, which is the release of gas. Excessive amounts of this gas can result in bloating and flatulence and affect gut "motility," contributing to constipation or diarrhea. The fermentation action of the gut bacteria figures prominently in the FODMAP diet theory.

How FODMAPs Cause Symptoms

FODMAPs are thought to contribute to digestive symptoms for some people because of the effects that they have within the digestive system. People with IBS have two main differences compared to those without IBS. The first is a problem with *motility*, resulting in symptoms of either constipation or diarrhea. The second problem is something called *visceral hypersensitivity*. A person with visceral hypersensitivity experiences pain and discomfort in the inner organs at a lower level of stimulation than does the average person. A diet high in FODMAP foods is thought to aggravate both of these problems.

What Does Motility Mean?
"Motility" is the term used by doctors and scientists to describe the speed and strength of muscle movement within the digestive tract. A motility disorder is one in which the muscles do not work smoothly and regularly. Fast motility propels stool too quickly through the intestines, resulting in diarrhea. Slow motility results in constipation's hard stools and infrequent bowel movements.

There are three factors attributed to the various FODMAPs that appear to trigger symptoms in people who are prone to motility problems and visceral hypersensitivity:

1. FODMAPs are poorly absorbed in the small intestine. This means that they are able to make their way into the large intestine, where they interact with gut bacteria.
2. To varying degrees, FODMAPs have an osmotic effect. This means that they increase the volume of water delivered from the small intestine into the large intestine. This is thought to contribute to the watery stools of diarrhea. This increased water volume also appears to trigger abdominal pain in susceptible individuals as the expanded volume of liquid puts pressure on the nerve cells within the intestinal lining.
3. Also to varying degrees, FODMAPs are rapidly fermented by gut bacteria. The output of this fermentation process is excessive intestinal gas, which can lead to bloating and flatulence. This excessive gas puts further pressure on the intestinal lining, contributing to abdominal pain.

It is important to note that FODMAPs are not the cause of digestive disorders. They are normal food components that provide a wide variety of health benefits. The problem with FODMAPs is only seen in individuals who already have motility dysfunction and visceral hypersensitivity, both of which are worsened by the excess pressure caused by the increased liquid and gas levels that these carbohydrates produce.

In the beginning, the diet requires that you avoid foods that you might eat regularly, even if they are healthy, because of their FODMAP composition. However, as you proceed with the diet, you will be able to reintroduce many foods once you identify which food components are troublesome for you. In addition, most people find that their tolerance for certain FODMAPs improves with time. Although the diet restricts many healthy foods, with careful planning you can follow a low-FODMAP diet and still eat enough of a variety of healthy foods that you can be assured that you are getting adequate nutrition.

FODMAP Research

FODMAP researchers used two different types of studies to confirm their initial theory. The first type of study involved people who had ileostomies. An ileostomy is the result of a surgical procedure in which the large intestine is removed. When a person has an ileostomy, the contents of the small intestine are diverted into a pouch worn on the outside of the body. FODMAP researchers analyzed the output of the ileum in people who had ileostomies to assess for the presence of FODMAPs. FODMAPs were present, which confirmed the hypothesis that they were not absorbed by the small intestine. In addition, the amount of FODMAPs present correlated with the amount of liquid being delivered from the small intestine. This confirmed the osmotic properties of the FODMAP carbohydrates.

QUESTION

Why don't FODMAPs cause symptoms in healthy people?
You may be very aware that you have a strong reaction to foods that other people seem to eat without a care. Although FODMAPs can cause the same physical reactions—fermentation and increased water output—within healthy people, there are factors within a person with IBS, not fully understood, that cause them to experience symptoms in response to these reactions.

The second type of study conducted involved testing breath hydrogen levels. Breath hydrogen is a measure of the amount of gas that is produced by gut bacteria through fermentation. IBS patients and healthy volunteers were placed on either high- or low-FODMAP diets. Results indicated that eating a high-FODMAP diet increases breath hydrogen levels, while a low-FODMAP diet produces significantly lower levels of breath hydrogen, regardless of whether or not a person had IBS. This led to a confirmation of the fermentative nature of FODMAPs.

FODMAP Load

Have you ever noticed that you can eat a food one day, yet feel miserable after eating it on a different day? This may be related to something called "FODMAP load," a key component to the low-FODMAP diet. FODMAP load has to do with the fact that the more FODMAPs that are eaten together, or within the same day, the more likely you are to have a problem. In other words, you may be able to tolerate smaller amounts of FODMAPs without having a problem. Add too many together, too soon, and symptoms will develop.

The nice thing about the notion of "load" is that you don't have to be too concerned if you inadvertently eat something that has a trace amount of a FODMAP you are restricting. And since anxiety is also a possible contributor to digestive distress, the last thing you need is to add unnecessary worry to the mix!

In the initial Elimination Phase of the diet, you won't have to focus on FODMAP load because you will be choosing to eat only foods that are low in FODMAPs. The notion of load will figure more prominently when you move past the Challenge Phase and start to expand the range of foods that you eat.

FODMAP sensitivity can change over time. Although the reason behind this is unclear, there is evidence that your ability to tolerate previously problematic food will increase. This means that you may find that you will be able to enjoy some of your favorite foods in the future without paying for them with digestive distress.

FODMAP Sensitivity

It is important to remember that not all FODMAPs cause symptoms in every IBS patient. People differ widely in their sensitivity to the various types of FODMAPs. You will learn how to identify which FODMAPs are problematic to you through the second phase of the diet. After initially following a completely low-FODMAP diet for a period of time, you will test foods from each of the FODMAP types and assess their effect on your system. This will ensure that you only restrict yourself from the foods that are truly troublesome for you.

FODMAP Types

In the FODMAP classification system, FODMAP carbohydrates are also broken down by type. Some of these groups might be familiar to you:

- Fructans
- GOS (galactooligosaccharides)
- Lactose
- Fructose
- Polyols

The components of these carbohydrate groups are found in many common foods. For example, fructans are found in garlic, onion, rye, and wheat. GOS are found in legumes and nuts. Lactose is found in milk products, while fructose is found in many fruits. Polyols are found in some artificial sweeteners, fruits such as blackberries, and vegetables such as cauliflower and mushrooms. It is also possible for a food to contain more than one FODMAP type.

FODMAP: The Acronym

To help you understand why you will or will not be eating certain foods, here is a closer look at each of the terms and types that make up the FODMAP acronym.

Fermentation

Fermentation is represented as the "F" in FODMAP. Fermentation is the result of gut bacteria interacting with carbohydrates, a process that triggers the release of several types of gases. These gases are either absorbed into the bloodstream or result in burping, flatulence, or bloating.

Fructans and GOS

Fructans and GOS are both types of oligosaccharides—the "O" in FOD-MAP. These carbohydrates are poorly digested by everyone, as humans lack the necessary enzymes to break them down and absorb their components into our bloodstream. Since they are not digested fully by the time they reach the large intestine, they are available to be fermented by the gut bacteria.

Fructans are found in wheat, many vegetables (most notably garlic and onions), and FOS (fructooligosaccharide) and inulin, both of which are common food additives. Fructans may be the biggest contributor to gut symptoms in our society as wheat, garlic, and onions figure prominently in most of the diets of people in the Western world.

ALERT

Watch out for hidden fructans in processed food products. Read ingredient labels carefully and don't buy any foods that contain FOS, chicory root extract (inulin), garlic powder, onion powder, and/or dehydrated vegetable powder.

GOS, sometimes called galactans, can be found in legumes, including beans, chickpeas, and lentils, and therefore often figure highly in Indian and Mexican cuisines as well as in the diets of vegetarians.

Lactose

Lactose is a disaccharide—the "D" in FODMAP. As you probably know, many people are lactose intolerant, a digestive problem also known as lactose malabsorption. Problems with lactose occur in individuals who lack enough of the enzyme lactase. Lactase is an enzyme essential for the digestion of lactose. Lactase breaks lactose down into two monosaccharides, glucose and galactose, so that they can be absorbed into the bloodstream by the small intestine. When there is a deficiency in lactase, lactose is not absorbed and is fermented by gut bacteria, resulting in symptoms.

Lactose malabsorption is more common in individuals who are American Indian, Asian, black, or Hispanic. Lactose malabsorption also increases with age due to a lower production of lactase. People with functional gastrointestinal disorders (FGIDs) like IBS and those who have an inflammatory bowel disease (IBD) demonstrate higher rates of lactose malabsorption.

Most people who have lactose malabsorption still produce some lactase and so can tolerate small amounts of lactose without experiencing digestive symptoms. In addition, dairy products differ in the amount of lactose that they contain. Therefore, certain dairy products are allowed as part of a low-FODMAP diet.

Lactose malabsorption can be identified through the use of a hydrogen breath test (HBT, which is explained later in this chapter). If possible, it is helpful if you can undergo such testing prior to starting a low-FODMAP diet. If you are not found to have lactose malabsorption you do not need to restrict yourself from eating lactose-containing foods during any phase of the diet.

What is a functional gastrointestinal disorder (FGID)?
A functional gastrointestinal disorder is one in which a person experiences symptoms related to how the digestive system is functioning, but no visible disease process or structural abnormality shows up in diagnostic testing. Without any measurable sign of disease, the diagnosis is made based on the symptom picture.

Fructose

Fructose is a monosaccharide—the "M" in FODMAP. Fructose is the sugar found in many fruits, honey, and high fructose corn syrup (HFCS). Fructose malabsorption is experienced by approximately one-third of all humans, with higher rates seen in those with an FGID or with Crohn's disease.

Fructose malabsorption is the result of fructose not being absorbed well at the level of the small intestine. In order for fructose to pass through the lining of the small intestine, it requires the presence of a transporter called GLUT-5. In some people, there is a lessened amount of this transporter, resulting in malabsorption.

Luckily, the extent of the malabsorption is strongly affected by the presence of glucose. When glucose is present, another transporter, known as GLUT-2, is activated, which facilitates the absorption of fructose. Therefore, foods that contain equal parts of fructose and glucose or have more glucose than fructose can be eaten in moderation without causing symptoms.

This factor plays strongly in the consideration of foods that are allowed in the low-FODMAP diet. For example, you might be surprised to see that sugar is allowed in the diet. This is because sugar has an equal amount of fructose and glucose. Generally, people who have IBS will have a problem with a food if the fructose level in the food exceeds the glucose level by more than 0.2 grams. You will not need to remember this, as the FODMAP researchers have done the math for you! On the other hand, there is a limit as to how much fructose your body can tolerate, regardless of the fructose/glucose ratio, so it is important not to eat too many fructose-containing foods in close proximity of one another.

Fructose malabsorption is different from hereditary fructose intolerance (HFI), a much more serious disorder. HFI is a genetic disorder typically diagnosed in infancy. Symptoms typically appear once the infant is given formula or baby food. HFI can vary in severity; at its worst, it can result in liver disease. Fructose malabsorption does not result in any danger to your health—only unwanted digestive symptoms.

Like lactose malabsorption, fructose malabsorption can be identified through the use of HBT, which is another reason why it is helpful to undergo such testing, if available, prior to starting on the low-FODMAP diet. This way you will know if you need to restrict fructose or if you can enjoy it through all phases of the diet.

Polyols

Polyols—the "P" in FODMAP—are sugar alcohols with scientific names that typically end in "-ol." Polyols are found naturally in some fruits and vegetables and are often used as artificial sweeteners. Polyol types include:

- Isomalt
- Maltitol
- Mannitol

- Polydextrose
- Sorbitol
- Xylitol

Polyol malabsorption is a quite common condition, present in more than half of all humans. In addition to contributing to excessive intestinal gas and bloating, polyols also have the dubious distinction as being strong contributors to diarrhea due to their laxative effect. As you follow the low-FODMAP diet, you will become very good at reading ingredient labels and looking for the presence of polyol artificial sweeteners.

Hydrogen Breath Testing

Hydrogen breath testing (HBT) is not mandated as part of the low-FODMAP diet. However, the developers of the diet strongly recommend HBT prior to starting the diet, as it will help you identify your own personal malabsorption problems. Unfortunately, availability of these tests varies widely by geographic location. In addition, many doctors question the validity of the testing. You can ask your doctor or do a web search to find out if the test is available in your area. Don't worry if you can't get the testing done—your individual malabsorption problems can also be identified through the process of elimination followed by challenging each of the various types of FODMAPs.

ESSENTIAL

HBT requires that you eat foods that are very low in FODMAPs for twenty-four hours prior to the test. This allows for a more accurate measure as to how your body responds to the sugar solutions that you are given to drink, as opposed to reacting to something you ate prior to the test.

If you would like to pursue HBT, it is helpful to understand how the testing works. Identification of malabsorption difficulties through HBT is possible because of the natural process of carbohydrate fermentation by gut bacteria. The byproduct of this fermentation is gas, including hydrogen and methane. Your body disposes of gas through burping, flatulence, or absorption in the bloodstream. Once it is in the blood, it is exhaled out of the body by the lungs. HBT is a way to measure the amount of gas that is produced by gut bacteria.

The staff at the test center will give you specific instructions about preparing for the test. On the day of the test, breath samples will be taken before and after you are given solutions to drink. There are a variety of sugars that can be tested through the use of HBT—fructose, glucose, lactose, lactulose, sorbitol, sucrose, and mannitol—but only one carbohydrate can be tested at a time. Everyone experiences fructan and GOS malabsorption, so there is no need for a test for these FODMAPs.

Samples of your breath will be collected for a few hours after you drink the test solution. The presence of hydrogen, or for some people, methane, in the breath will confirm that the carbohydrate was available to the gut bacteria for fermentation. This means that it was not absorbed at the level of the small intestine, and a malabsorption is diagnosed.

SIBO and FODMAPs

SIBO (small intestine bacterial overgrowth) is a condition in which excessive amounts of gut bacteria are present within the small intestine. In a healthy individual, the small intestine has a natural "cleansing wave," in which the muscles of the small intestine flush out its contents at regular intervals into the large intestine. SIBO is typically seen in individuals who have had something happen to impair this cleansing wave, e.g., abdominal surgery or Crohn's disease. This allows for an accumulation of bacteria within the small intestine. Since the symptoms of SIBO—abdominal pain, bloating, constipation, diarrhea, and excessive gas—mimic the symptoms of IBS, some researchers believe that SIBO may be an underlying cause of IBS in some individuals.

Diagnosis of SIBO

Similar to fructose and lactose malabsorption, SIBO is diagnosed through the use of HBT. If you are undergoing HBT for SIBO, you will be given a solution of either glucose or lactulose to drink. Since it takes these sugars approximately two hours to reach the gut bacteria in the large intestine, any significant gas increase seen in your breath before the ninety-minute mark suggests that bacteria within the small intestine were responsible for fermenting the tested sugar.

SIBO and IBS

SIBO researchers have sought to understand why bacteria would be present in the small intestine in some people who have IBS. One theory is that a bad bout of a stomach "flu" damaged the muscles of the small intestine. This would serve as a possible explanation for the phenomenon of post-infectious IBS, in which a person develops IBS after a bad stomach infection. Another theory is that stress, as part of the body's natural stress response, slows down the action of the cleansing wave. This would account for the fact that many people find that their IBS is worsened when they are under stress.

FACT

The SIBO theory addresses the bewildering fact that IBS can cause problems with both constipation and diarrhea. It is thought that different bacteria may play a role in each problem. Patients who show more methane in the breath during SIBO testing are more likely to have constipation as their predominant bowel syndrome, while patients who show more hydrogen in the breath are more likely to experience chronic diarrhea.

Support for the SIBO/IBS connection comes from research that shows that people who have IBS are more likely than healthy individuals to show the presence of fermentation within the ninety-minute mark during the HBT. Further support for the theory comes from the fact that many IBS patients report a decrease in their symptoms when they are treated with a specific type of antibiotic used as a treatment for SIBO.

The SIBO theory is not without controversy. Some researchers question the reliability of the breath test, while others have concerns about the reliability and safety of the antibiotics used as a SIBO treatment.

SIBO Treatment

The primary treatment of SIBO is the use of antibiotics that have been chosen specifically because they are not absorbed in the stomach like most antibiotics. This allows the antibiotic to arrive at the small intestine and eradicate any bacteria lurking there. Although many doctors are routinely prescribing antibiotics to IBS patients thought to have SIBO, at the time of this writing no antibiotic has yet to be approved by the FDA for the treatment of IBS.

There is no definitive diet for SIBO. The general recommendation is that you not restrict your intake of carbohydrates while on the antibiotic, so that the antibiotic will have a healthy population of bacteria within the small intestine to attack. After the SIBO has been eradicated, you may be instructed to minimize your intake of foods that are not well absorbed.

An important aspect of SIBO treatment concerns the operation of the cleansing wave. In order to maximize the effectiveness of this cleansing process in keeping the small intestine free from an overabundance of bacteria, you should stick to three meals a day and avoid "grazing." Restricting the number of times that you eat is important because the cleansing wave is most effective when you are not eating.

ALERT

If you have had the experience of seeing a dramatic improvement in your IBS symptoms when you have taken antibiotics for an unrelated health problem, you should talk to your doctor about being tested for SIBO. You may then be a candidate for antibiotic treatment to clean up the bacterial overgrowth in your small intestine.

SIBO or FODMAPs

For a definitive diagnosis of SIBO, you would have to undergo breath testing. However, your body will give you some clues to help you to figure out whether you have a problem with SIBO or with FODMAPs:

- With SIBO, you will more likely experience symptoms within ninety minutes of eating a particular food.
- FODMAPs generally take at least two hours before causing symptoms, as they need to make their way into the large intestine before being fermented by gut bacteria.
- If you experience symptoms in response to all types of carbohydrates, even those that are not classified as FODMAPs, you are more likely to

have SIBO. This is because bacteria in the small intestine have access to all of the foods that you eat. When no SIBO is present, only the carbohydrates that are not absorbed by the small intestine are labeled as FODMAPs.

As of now, there is scant research as to the use of the low-FODMAP diet for SIBO. Therefore, if you are diagnosed with SIBO, you should not start the low-FODMAP diet until you have finished the course of antibiotics. Once the SIBO is resolved, you may find that the low-FODMAP diet helps with maintenance, but be sure to get clearance from your doctor first.

Where Does Fiber Fit In?

A typical scenario for a newly diagnosed IBS patient is to be told by her doctor to go home and increase her intake of dietary fiber. All too often, this results in a worsening of symptoms! For this reason, many people who have IBS become fearful of fiber because they associate it with an increase in symptoms. With an understanding of the role that FODMAPs play in terms of gut symptoms, you now know why this was often the case: Many high-fiber foods are also high in FODMAPs.

QUESTION

What is fiber?
Fiber is the part of plant food that is indigestible. Fiber is classified as soluble and insoluble. Soluble fiber dissolves in water, adding bulk to the stool and keeping it soft. Insoluble fiber does not draw water into itself, thus adding to stool bulk. Both types of fiber are essential for your digestive and overall health.

The beauty of the FODMAP approach is that the troublesome aspects of fiber have been clearly identified and eliminated. This will provide you with the confidence to consume high-fiber foods without worry, as long as they are low in FODMAPs or have been identified as containing FODMAPs that are not a problem for you. In fact, research on the low-FODMAP diet has shown that it improves the consistency of stool in IBS patients, regardless of whether the primary problem is constipation or diarrhea.

Diet Overview

The research-based way to follow a low-FODMAP diet is divided into the Elimination Phase and the Challenge Phase. In the Elimination Phase, you will follow a diet that consists only of low-FODMAP foods. This phase will last for four to eight weeks. Following the elimination diet for a full eight weeks optimizes the chances that you will experience the full benefit of the diet and increases the likelihood that you will be able to tolerate additional FODMAPs during the Challenge Phase.

In the Challenge Phase, you will systematically introduce each type of FODMAP back into your diet and evaluate how your digestive system responds. This process may take several weeks or months as you gather information regarding what foods your body can and cannot tolerate.

Once you have completed the Challenge Phase, you will settle into a regular way of eating that consists of foods that your body is comfortable with. Through the food challenges, you will have a good sense of the variety of foods that you can eat. As time passes, it is best that you intermittently retest a FODMAP type that has shown itself to be problematic in the past. You may find that your ability to tolerate previously troublesome FODMAPs has improved. It is important to remember that the overall goal of the diet is to be able to eat a very wide range of foods while keeping symptoms quiet. Over time, you may find that there are only a few of the higher-FODMAP foods that you need to stay away from.

Not a Traditional Diet

It is important to keep in mind that the low-FODMAP diet is a therapeutic way of eating, not a diet in our traditional "weight loss" sense. You will not necessarily lose weight on this diet. You may—but only because you will perhaps be eating healthier foods than you were eating before starting the diet.

There is no "one size fits all" aspect to the low-FODMAP diet. Therefore, there is no need to stick to a strict eating plan, other than being sure to eat only low-FODMAP foods (or foods that have been identified as safe for you through HBT) in the Elimination Phase. Every person's body is different, and therefore levels of tolerance of FODMAP-containing foods will vary widely. You are encouraged to work closely with your own body (or with a dietitian or health coach) to determine which foods work or don't work for you.

The low-FODMAP diet is also not as strict as a gluten-free diet is for a person with celiac disease. People who have celiac disease can never eat foods containing gluten, as they will be putting their bodies at risk for serious health problems if they do so. If you "slip" or "go off" the low-FODMAP diet, you will not be putting your health in any danger. You may suffer the consequences of once again experiencing the symptoms that prompted you to start the diet in the first place, but you will not be harming yourself.

Disclaimer

The information in this book is included for educational purposes only and should not be used as a substitute for diagnosis and treatment rendered by a qualified medical professional. The low-FODMAP diet is a fledgling science; all information presented in this book is based on the information available at the time of its writing. Information about the diet and the food recommendations included in this book are subject to change. In addition, the diet has only been evaluated for effectiveness for individuals who received support from a dietitian. Thus, no guarantees can be made as to symptom response resulting from following the book's recommendations. Last, all recipes in this book were created using low-FODMAP ingredients (as identified at the time of this writing), but they have not been tested for their overall FODMAP content.

CHAPTER 2

The Low-FODMAP Diet for Digestive Problems

The low-FODMAP diet was designed to offer IBS patients a way of eating that does not aggravate symptoms. It does not necessarily "cure" the underlying problem, but it has been shown to be effective in reducing abdominal pain, bloating, flatulence, constipation, and diarrhea. There is also emerging evidence that the diet may be helpful for people who don't have IBS, yet experience these same symptoms on a regular basis.

Do You Have IBS?

If you have already been given a diagnosis, feel free to skim through the next few sections. However, often people wonder if they have IBS. Their intestines are acting up, but they haven't yet talked to a doctor about it. If that is the case for you, it would be helpful to learn more about the disorder so you know the right questions to ask your doctor at your next appointment.

Doctors have a set of diagnostic criteria, called the Rome III criteria, for making a firm diagnosis of IBS. The Rome criteria require that a person experiences abdominal pain or discomfort along with a marked change in bowel habit for at least six months. In addition, symptoms must have occurred on at least three days of at least three months. In addition, at least two of the following must apply:

- Pain is relieved by a bowel movement.
- The onset of pain symptoms is associated with a change in the frequency of bowel movements.
- The onset of pain symptoms is related to a change in the way stool appears.

ESSENTIAL

If you are experiencing chronic digestive difficulties, it is essential that you speak with your doctor. Many other health problems have symptoms that are quite similar to IBS. It is important to ensure that you have an accurate diagnosis so that you will be assured that you are getting optimal treatment before you start to follow a low-FODMAP diet.

In the real world, doctors tend to give the diagnosis to anyone who has chronic digestive symptoms without any identifiable reason, regardless of whether or not the symptoms meet the Rome III criteria.

Symptoms of IBS

Typically IBS symptoms consist of abdominal pain (including cramping and spasms), gas and bloating, and constipation or diarrhea. Constipation is defined as three or fewer bowel movements a week, with hard, dry stools and possible straining during bowel movements. Diarrhea is defined as three or more bowel movements a day, with loose, watery stools, and feelings of urgency. Other IBS symptoms include the sensation of incomplete evacuation and mucus passed along with stool.

Many people who have IBS report a wide variety of other symptoms that seem to go along with their IBS. Some of these symptoms are also gastrointestinal, such as nausea and heartburn. Other symptoms include dizziness, fatigue, head, back, and overall muscle pain, heart palpitations, and urinary problems.

Many women find that their digestive symptoms are very much related to their menstrual cycle. They may experience a worsening of their symptoms prior to or during the days that they have their period. Researchers do not yet have any solid answers to explain why this happens.

FACT

Some people may experience symptoms similar to a fainting episode during bowel movements. This includes sweating, feeling like one is going to pass out, and in rare cases, actually fainting. This phenomenon is related to what is called the "vasovagal reflex," a response in which your vagus nerves (nerves which carry information from your organs to your brain) trigger rapid changes in your cardiovascular system, including a sudden drop in blood pressure and heart rate.

Causes of IBS

Don't listen to the people who tell you that "IBS is all in your head"! Although no one knows for sure why some people develop IBS, there are real biological changes involved. Here are some of the primary areas that scientists are exploring as they try to figure out what is going on:

- **Bacteria:** Researchers are looking into the role that bacteria play in contributing to IBS symptoms. This research includes a look at the phenomenon of post-infectious IBS, a validation of the role of SIBO, and the search for a more in-depth understanding of dysbiosis. (See Chapter 1 for more about SIBO and dysbiosis.)

- **Inflammation:** Although with IBS there is no visible inflammation in the intestinal lining such as that seen in inflammatory bowel disease (IBD), researchers are looking into the possibility that there is a state of microscopic inflammation.
- **Brain-Gut Connection:** There are many interconnections between your brain and your digestive system. Researchers are looking into dysfunction among these pathways, as well as problems with specific neurotransmitters (chemicals that convey information from one nerve cell to the next).

The Role of Stress

As you may have experienced, often IBS symptoms are worse when a person is under stress. The connection between stress and digestive functioning is deep and complex, and is very much related to your body's natural response to perceived threats.

When we were evolving as a species, our bodies needed a way to deal with unexpected threats to our survival. In other words, if we came out of a cave and were faced with a hungry predator, our bodies had to have the ability to either fight off the attacker or run to safety. Hence, the "fight or flight" response. This response causes the body to maximize the resources necessary for breathing and for muscle strength and to divert resources away from digestion. When you are fighting for your life, digesting lunch becomes less important.

The stress response thus can have a significant impact on how your intestines are functioning. In modern life, we experience more daily, chronic stress than did our predecessors (who had to deal with occasional extreme stress like hungry lions!). This continual activation of the stress response can contribute to chronic digestive problems.

ESSENTIAL

You can learn how to reduce the impact of the stress response on your body. Relaxation exercises, such as visualization, deep breathing, and progressive muscle relaxation, all help to send the signal to your body that the alarm bells can be turned off. Regular practice of yoga, tai chi, and/or meditation can also offset the effect of stress on your body.

Stress alone does not account for the problems behind IBS, as many people who are under a great deal of stress don't experience IBS symptoms. New research is beginning to shed light on the effect of stress on the balance of gut bacteria, which in turn may contribute to inflammation.

Diagnostic Tests for IBS

The diagnosis of IBS is based on symptom report and is made after ruling out other disorders. Typically, your doctor will conduct a comprehensive physical exam, order blood work, and ask you for a stool sample to look for the presence of rectal bleeding. Depending on your symptom picture, the doctor may recommend that you undergo further testing, such as a colonoscopy or endoscopy. These tests are not essential for a diagnosis of IBS, but rather are used to rule out other reasons behind your symptoms. The Rome III criteria were designed to come up with a definitive diagnosis of IBS so as to prevent having patients undergo unnecessary diagnostic procedures.

Food Allergy and Intolerance

Since the low-FODMAP diet focuses on the relationship between food and digestive symptoms, it is a good idea to be educated regarding food allergies and food intolerance. Understanding how they differ will help you to make a decision as to whether the low-FODMAP diet is right for you or whether you should be pursuing a different course of action.

Food Allergy

A food allergy is an immune system reaction to a particular food that is not harmful to most people. When a person has a food allergy, eating even a small amount of the offending food will prompt the immune system to release chemicals that cause a variety of symptoms. You are probably familiar with typical allergy symptoms—hives, itching, and lip swelling—in addition to the more serious symptoms of difficulty breathing and swelling of the throat. Food allergies can also create gastrointestinal symptoms such as vomiting, diarrhea, and/or abdominal pain. The most common food allergens include eggs, fish and shellfish, milk, peanuts, soy, tree nuts, and wheat.

In an allergic reaction, the body produces antibodies when it encounters what it perceives as an invader. These antibodies are known as Immunoglobulin E, or IgE. The IgE reaction triggers the release of histamine and other chemicals, causing allergy symptoms. IgE release can be identified through the use of allergy tests, thus helping to confirm a diagnosis of a food allergy.

Food Intolerance

A food intolerance, also known as a food sensitivity, is when a person has a negative reaction to a food without it being an allergy. An allergy involves a clear reaction on the part of the immune system (with an IgE response), while a food intolerance is a reaction on the part of the gastrointestinal system (although there may still be some immune system involvement). Therefore, symptoms of a food intolerance are often gastrointestinal in nature. Researchers have attempted to use an IgG, Immunoglobin G, as a measure of intolerance, but that does not appear to be as reliable a marker as IgE is for food allergy.

FACT

Food intolerance symptoms may not always be gastrointestinal in nature. Researchers who are looking into something called "intestinal permeability," more commonly referred to as "leaky gut syndrome," theorize that an immune system reaction triggered by a food intolerance may be behind a variety of human ailments. Possible conditions of this type include acne, allergies, autism, and diabetes.

Because there are no definitive tests for food intolerance, food intolerance is typically identified through the use of an elimination diet, similar to that of the Elimination Phase of the low-FODMAP diet. An elimination diet requires that (with your doctor's permission) you refrain from eating any foods with a reputation for intolerance (e.g., gluten, dairy, soy) for a period of two to eight weeks. During that time, you will keep track of your symptoms. At the end of the elimination period, you will slowly introduce these foods back into your diet, one at a time, to evaluate your reaction to them. An intolerance will be identified if you experience symptoms directly in response to a food that was recently reintroduced. Research has shown that elimination diets can be effective in reducing some IBS symptoms.

Low-FODMAP Diet or Elimination Diet?

Many people strongly advocate for the use of an elimination diet for IBS. Since an elimination diet can also reduce symptoms, it is natural to wonder whether one should be giving that a try rather than the low-FODMAP diet. A decision such as this is a personal one, and one that should be discussed with your doctor. The advantages of the low-FODMAP diet over an elimination diet is that it has significant research support for its effectiveness. It also involves a process of careful identification of food triggers, thus reducing the risk that you will unnecessarily avoid foods.

Celiac Disease and Gluten Sensitivity

The food intolerance that is currently getting the most attention is gluten. Celiac disease, an autoimmune condition triggered by the consumption of gluten, used to be viewed as a very rare condition. However, this is no longer the case. This rising rate of celiac disease diagnoses has resulted in an increase in the amount and types of gluten-free food options that are readily available. If you have already been screened for celiac disease, feel free to skip this section. However, if you have not yet been tested, it is essential that you become educated about this serious digestive disorder.

What Is Celiac Disease?

Celiac disease is an autoimmune condition in which the body's immune system reacts to the presence of gluten. Gluten is a protein found in products containing barley, rye, and wheat. When a person with celiac disease eats something containing gluten, the immune system attacks and damages the villi lining the small intestine. (See the sidebar in Chapter 1 for more about the villi.) The damage to the villi prevents the body from being able to absorb important nutrients. This can result in serious health problems and a wide variety of symptoms. Celiac disease is diagnosed according to initial blood screening, followed by an endoscopy with a biopsy of the lining of the small intestine.

Celiac Disease and IBS

The gastrointestinal symptoms of celiac disease are very similar to those of IBS—abdominal pain, bloating, and diarrhea. Research indicates that IBS patients are at significantly higher risk for celiac disease. Therefore, if you have IBS, it is essential that you be screened for celiac disease. If you are subsequently diagnosed with celiac disease, you must follow a strict gluten-free diet for the rest of your life.

ALERT

In order to receive an accurate test result from celiac disease screening, you must be eating gluten at the time of the test. The tests are only accurate if gluten is in your system. Therefore, do not restrict gluten from your diet until after the testing is complete.

What Is Gluten Sensitivity?

Gluten sensitivity is a condition in which a person reacts negatively to foods containing gluten, but who does not have celiac disease. When a person has a gluten sensitivity, the immune system does not attack the villi, so there is no concern about damage to the small intestine. Unlike a person with celiac disease, a person with gluten sensitivity can eat gluten without the concern of permanent damage, but may suffer the consequence of undesirable symptoms.

FACT

Due to a growing recognition of the high number of IBS patients who react poorly to gluten, researchers have come up with the term "non-celiac gluten sensitivity (NCGS)" as a diagnosis for such patients. NCGS is theorized to be a subset of IBS.

The symptoms of gluten sensitivity may be gastrointestinal in nature, with symptoms such as abdominal pain, constipation, and diarrhea. There is also the theory that a gluten sensitivity may cause other symptoms throughout the body—symptoms such as brain fog, fatigue, headaches, and joint pain. Like other sensitivities and intolerances, a gluten sensitivity is typically identified through the use of an elimination diet and challenge test.

The Low-FODMAP Diet and Gluten

In the low-FODMAP diet, gluten is not allowed. However, this is not because of the gluten itself, but rather the level of fructans within gluten-containing foods. There are two perks that come from this. The first is that if you have a gluten sensitivity, the restriction of gluten from your diet will mean that you should feel significantly better! The second perk is that the abundance of gluten-free options now available in stores and restaurants helps to make it easier to follow the low-FODMAP diet.

Alternative IBS Treatments

As of now there is no one standard treatment protocol for IBS. You are also probably well aware that there is also no known "cure." Frustratingly, the goal of standard medical treatment has historically been one of symptom management. Doctors typically recommend the use of medications, fiber supplements, and over-the-counter products (OTCs). There is also research support for the usefulness of some mind-body treatments; in particular, hypnotherapy and psychotherapy.

Medications

There are a wide variety of medications that doctors may prescribe for IBS. Most of these medications are not specifically designed to treat IBS, but rather address its symptoms. Antispasmodics are prescribed to reduce abdominal pain and cramping; antidepressants may be prescribed due to their pain-relieving qualities and their effect on gut motility; and antibiotics may be prescribed for the treatment of SIBO. There are also a number of new medications being designed specifically to treat IBS. These medications target specific neurotransmitters and their receptor cells within the digestive tract.

Fiber Supplements

Many doctors recommend that IBS patients increase their intake of dietary fiber through the use of a fiber supplement. This is because fiber helps to resolve both constipation and diarrhea due to its effect on stool formation. However, increasing fiber can be troublesome for some people due to gut fermentation. One fiber supplement that is permitted on a low-FODMAP diet is Citrucel, as it is made of methylcellulose, which is nonfermentable.

Over-the-Counter Products (OTCs)

Because the current medical treatments for IBS are limited, IBS patients often turn to over-the-counter products for symptom relief. People with diarrhea-predominant IBS (IBS-D) are likely to use loperamide in order to try to reduce symptoms, while people with constipation-predominant IBS (IBS-C) often use stool softeners. Peppermint oil has received some research support for its effectiveness in reducing abdominal pain and cramping. There are also a wide variety of herbal remedies and vitamins that IBS patients have turned to in the pursuit of symptom relief.

ALERT

Do not take any OTC substance, including herbal remedies and vitamins, without first checking with your doctor. Not all "natural remedies" are safe, and others can be problematic for those with specific health conditions. Your doctor is in the best position to evaluate whether a product is safe for you, given your medical history.

Probiotics, often referred to as "friendly bacteria," can be taken in supplement form. These bacteria strains are thought to encourage a favorable balance of the bacteria within the gut flora, reducing inflammation, supporting the immune system, and reducing excessive fermentation. People often wonder which probiotic supplement they should take. Due to the vast number of types of bacterial strains, it is hard to conduct definitive research studies regarding which supplement is best.

Most studies do indicate a favorable effect of probiotics on IBS symptoms. It may also be reassuring to know that probiotics are generally well tolerated, meaning that they rarely result in any negative side effects. (Probiotics should not be taken if you have a weakened immune system or any serious health problem.) It is generally recommended that a probiotic be taken for four weeks to assess its effectiveness.

QUESTION

What about probiotics in foods?
Probiotics can be found in some foods. The low-FODMAP diet does not allow for foods containing lactose; therefore yogurt products and kefir made from regular milk need to be avoided. Soy yogurt and kefir are also not allowed. Lactose-free or coconut-based yogurt and kefir are acceptable. Probiotics can also be found in fermented vegetables. As long as the base vegetable is low-FODMAP, such foods will most likely be well tolerated.

Mind-Body Treatments

Due to the close relationship between our brains and our guts, some IBS symptom relief can be found through the use of mind-body treatments. The two with the most research support in terms of effectiveness are hypnotherapy and cognitive-behavioral therapy (CBT). If you want to try hypnotherapy, make sure you go to a qualified professional. Hypnotherapy involves bringing you into a trance state, which can be deeply relaxing. While in this state, the hypnotherapist makes suggestions to address specific areas of concern; in this context, digestive functioning. CBT is a type of psychotherapy in which you would be taught how to change unhealthy ways of thinking and learn new ways of dealing with situations. The focus of CBT with a person who has IBS would be to decrease anxiety-provoking thoughts and teach anxiety management strategies.

The Low-FODMAP Diet for IBS

The low-FODMAP diet is the first diet ever to have research support for its effectiveness in reducing IBS symptoms of pain, gas, bloating, constipation, and diarrhea. It should come as quite a relief to you to hear that the diet is estimated to be effective for 75 to 86 percent of IBS patients. This is great news! Clinical studies report that positive results of the diet on IBS symptoms are typically seen after four weeks of adherence, though many people say they feel better within the first week of trying the diet.

Not surprisingly, sticking to the diet is very important in terms of achieving symptom relief. Therefore, for best results, you should try to do the full Elimination Phase to start. Again, no need to panic if this option is not for you—there are other ways to benefit from the diet that don't involve a strict restriction of all of your favorite foods. If you like the idea of following the full research-based diet but are concerned that the Elimination Phase might be too hard, you may want to consider working with a dietitian or health coach, either of whom will help to support you in making these changes to your everyday diet.

The effectiveness of the low-FODMAP diet on easing constipation may seem surprising. After all, part of the theory behind the diet is that there is an increase in fluid within the intestines caused by carbohydrates with osmotic properties. It would therefore seem that restricting such FODMAPs would result in a lower fluid level, exacerbating constipation. However, that does not always seem to be the case.

ALERT

Some people who typically experienced chronic diarrhea prior to the diet may find themselves with the opposite problem once they begin following this plan. If you experience constipation, be sure that you are eating plenty of high-fiber, but allowed, vegetables, fruits, and whole grains, as well as drinking plenty of water. A nonfermentable fiber supplement, such as Citrucel, may also be helpful.

Researchers are not completely sure what the mechanism is behind the improvement in constipation as a result of the diet. One theory is that as people follow the low-FODMAP diet, they may actually be taking in more dietary fiber than they were eating prior to the diet, improving the makeup of the stool. Another theory has to do with methane production. There is evidence that methane production, as the result of fermentation of carbohydrates by gut bacteria, is related to a reduction in gut motility and harder stools. The low-FODMAP diet may reduce the output of methane, therefore easing constipation.

The Low-FODMAP Diet for Other Digestive Problems

Most of the research on the low-FODMAP diet has been focused on its benefits for people with IBS. However, its effectiveness in reducing digestive symptoms have prompted researchers to explore the effect of the diet on other health conditions, most notably IBD and celiac disease.

Inflammatory Bowel Disease (IBD)

The inflammatory bowel diseases are Crohn's disease and ulcerative colitis. Some studies have shown that people whose IBD is in remission still exhibit IBS-like symptoms such as bloating and watery diarrhea. People with Crohn's disease appear to be at higher risk for fructose malabsorption, and those with ulcerative colitis may be at higher risk for lactose malabsorption. There is evidence that the low-FODMAP diet can reduce gut symptoms for up to 70 percent of IBD patients who exhibit ongoing digestive symptoms when their disease is in remission. If you are receiving the proper treatment for IBD, but still have symptoms, speak to your doctor about whether it would be okay for you to give the low-FODMAP diet a try.

Celiac Disease

It is possible for a person with celiac disease to either have IBS or to simply continue to experience digestive symptoms even when following a strict gluten-free diet. There is not yet a lot of research on the subject, but there are indications that if you fit into this category, your symptoms will be eased by the low-FODMAP diet.

Other Functional Gastrointestinal Disorders

A "functional" disorder is one in which there is a problem with the way that a system is functioning, but no visible disease process can be identified through testing. Sometimes people experience chronic digestive symptoms, not explained by the presence of disease, that don't meet the criteria for IBS. These include functional abdominal pain (more common in children), functional bloating, functional constipation (also known as chronic idiopathic constipation—idiopathic meaning "of unknown cause"), and functional diarrhea. Although research on the effectiveness of the low-FODMAP diet on these specific FGIDs is scarce, it is likely that individuals with these disorders would have a similar response as do those with classic IBS.

Before You Start the Diet

The low-FODMAP diet is not a temporary "fad diet." Instead, it is a scientific approach to ensure that the foods you are eating are well tolerated by your body. As such, it is a diet to be well prepared for. As eager as you may be to start the diet, there are a variety of things to consider and arrange for prior to embarking on the first phase.

See Your Doctor

Before you begin the diet, it is essential that you discuss the diet with your doctor. Your doctor is in the best position to ascertain whether the diet is safe for you. Of utmost importance is that you are correctly diagnosed. Since other health disorders can cause many of the same symptoms of IBS, it is essential that these be ruled out to ensure that you are receiving proper treatment. Your doctor will also make the determination as to which diagnostic tests need to be done before you start the diet.

Diagnostic Testing

As discussed earlier in the chapter, it is essential to rule out the presence of celiac disease prior to starting the diet. As you now know, celiac disease requires a 100 percent restriction of all foods containing any level of gluten. It is also essential to have a definitive diagnosis of celiac disease so that you can be screened for nutritional deficits and the presence of other disorders relating to celiac disease. Since the accuracy of celiac testing requires that you eat gluten, and the low-FODMAP diet restricts gluten, you need to be screened for celiac before starting the diet.

If hydrogen breath testing (HBT) is available in your area, it would be advisable to test for the presence of fructose, lactose, and/or polyol malabsorption. These tests are not essential, as such malabsorption can be identified in the Challenge Phase of the diet, but having them done before you start will make the diet so much easier for you. In addition, if your symptoms include a lot of gas and bloating, and these symptoms tend to show up within the first hour and a half after eating, you may want to also talk to your doctor about undergoing HBT for the presence of SIBO.

Change Your Fiber Supplement

If you have been taking a fiber supplement regularly, it is advisable to switch to Citrucel prior to starting the diet, as Citrucel is nonfermentable. Since fiber changes can cause an increase in symptoms, it is best to take the time to slowly decrease your original fiber supplement intake, while slowly increasing your intake of Citrucel.

Cut Back on Coffee

Coffee contains GOS (galactooligosaccharides) in small amounts. (See Chapter 1 for more about GOS.) Due to the effect of FODMAP load, too much coffee can be problematic. You should drink no more than one cup of coffee a day on a low-FODMAP diet.

Because reducing the amount of coffee that you drink means you are also reducing the amount of caffeine that you are taking in, you will want to wean off coffee gradually to avoid caffeine withdrawal symptoms, such as headaches. For best results, take the time to cut back by one-half cup each day until you get down to the allowed one cup per day.

Unfortunately, you do not have the luxury of weaning yourself onto decaffeinated coffee, as that too has some FODMAP content. You can switch to black or green tea, which contain some caffeine. Black tea should only be weakly brewed to avoid an excess of FODMAPs.

Tell People

Although most people with IBS find the disorder quite embarrassing and therefore hard to talk about, it will help your adherence to the diet if you tell the closest people in your life about it. No need to go into lengthy detail—keep it simple! All you have to say is that your doctor recommended that you follow a particular diet for some stomach problems. Attributing the diet to a physician recommendation carries a little weight, which might encourage others to be more respectful of your needs.

On the other hand, if you feel comfortable doing so, by all means tell people that you have IBS! Seeing as it affects up to 20 percent of the population, chances are good that as you tell others, they may reveal that they too are struggling with the disorder.

Get Dietary Assistance

The low-FODMAP diet was designed to be used under the guidance of a qualified dietitian. Dietitians are professionals who are trained in the science of food and nutrition. Often they have specialized training for supporting people who have specific health issues, such as digestive problems or diabetes. Ideally, you would want to find a dietitian who is quite familiar with the low-FODMAP diet.

QUESTION

Can a health coach help?
Yes, a health coach is an appropriate alternative to a dietitian. Health coaches are also trained in nutrition, although the course of study is not as rigorous as that of a dietitian. Health coaches are more likely to offer a holistic approach for helping individuals resolve their health concerns.

The advantage of working with a supportive professional while on the low-FODMAP diet is to get assurance that you are meeting all of your nutritional needs. Any diet of restriction runs the risk of nutritional deficiencies, and the low-FODMAP diet is no exception. Eating as wide a variety of foods as you can tolerate will minimize this risk. If you are already working with a professional but he or she does not have experience with the diet, hand that person this book!

Start a Symptom Diary

A funny thing about human beings is that once they start to feel better, they tend to forget how bad they felt prior. Start a Symptom Diary now so that you can judge your progress symptom-wise as you make your way through the diet.

DAILY SYMPTOM DIARY			
Date	Foods Eaten	Other Factors	Symptoms
Breakfast			
Snack			
Lunch			
Snack			
Dinner			
Dessert/Snack			

The column labeled "Other Factors" is a good place to record any extenuating circumstances that might contribute to your symptoms. For example, feeling stressed, skipping a meal, or, if you are a woman, being at a particular point in your menstrual cycle may all affect how your digestive system is operating apart from the food you are eating.

Diet Options

You will need to decide if you are going to follow the full diet—in other words, go through the Elimination Phase, followed by the Challenge Phase—or try one of two alternative methods. Alternatives include either restricting one FODMAP group at a time or taking a more casual approach to restriction. Although a full elimination can be challenging, its advantages certainly outweigh the convenience of the alternative approaches.

Advantages of the Full Elimination Approach

The full FODMAP elimination approach is firmly backed by research supporting its effectiveness. This approach also maximizes your chances to experience a complete (and highly welcomed!) sense of symptom relief that may come about by a total elimination of high-FODMAP foods. Following a full Elimination Phase will maximize your ability to tolerate foods that might have been problematic for you prior to starting the diet, allowing for a greater variety of foods over the long haul. In other words, if you restrict in the beginning there may be less restriction going forward. Last, although further research is needed, it is possible that the Elimination Phase helps to actually "heal the gut" through an improvement in the balance of gut bacteria.

The One-by-One Approach

The first alternative involves eliminating one FODMAP group at a time and assessing the effect of this dietary change on symptoms. The downside of this approach is that it may take longer for you to feel the relief that comes from eliminating the FODMAP groups that are problematic for you. However, because this approach involves some scientific detective work, you will still gain a knowledge of your own particular sensitivities, just as you would if you faithfully followed the full elimination option.

The Casual Approach

The low-FODMAP diet was developed to include a full Elimination Phase. However, in real life, many people follow a more casual approach in which they try their best to avoid eating high-FODMAP foods, eating more low-FODMAP foods instead. Although there is no research support for a casual approach, many IBS patients report that they experience a reduction in their IBS symptoms when they follow this approach. The upside is obvious in that this approach involves the least amount of restriction of the three. However, a major downside is that you may never experience the full benefit that comes from a complete restriction of high-FODMAP foods. Another downside is that you might be unnecessarily restricting certain foods without knowing for sure that they are problematic. The biggest risk to this approach is that it may not meet your full nutritional needs. However, this casual approach is an option if your IBS symptoms are not too severe or you really believe that you cannot adhere to either the Elimination/Challenge or the one-by-one approaches. It is best if you discuss your options with your physician.

The Low-FODMAP Diet for Kids

The low-FODMAP diet can be appropriate for children. It is first essential that your child have a full medical workup to ensure an accurate diagnosis and appropriate treatment. It is also highly advisable that you work with a dietitian to make sure that your child is getting all of the nutrients needed for proper growth and optimal health.

For some children, the total Elimination Phase may be unworkable. In that case, you may find it more practical to follow one of the alternative options for the diet. You can discuss the options with your child's doctor to ascertain which approach will be most appropriate for your child.

CHAPTER 3

The Elimination Phase

It's time to get started! In this initial phase, you'll eliminate all high-FODMAP foods from your diet. At first, this will require careful monitoring and preparation of the foods that you eat. You will need to change your normal shopping list and think more carefully about which foods to order in restaurants. But once you have a few basic recipes in your repertoire, you'll find it gets much easier. And you'll also have the extra payoff of feeling much better!

Elimination Phase Overview

The Elimination Phase of the diet typically lasts four to eight weeks. Without argument, this is certainly the strictest phase of the diet. Many foods that you typically eat will now be off-limits. But don't worry; although you will have to change the way you eat, you will still be able to eat lots of delicious foods! Also, you'll find that there are many substitutes you can use so you can still enjoy your favorite recipes. Starting with Chapter 6 of this book, you'll find recipes for all kinds of entrées, snacks, and even desserts. Every one of these recipes is appropriate for the Elimination Phase.

Although the lists of "no" and "yes" foods may seem a little overwhelming at first, with practice you'll find that it becomes almost second nature to know which foods are on the allowed and restricted lists.

ESSENTIAL

The scientists at Monash University have developed an app called "the Monash University LOW FODMAP diet" app, for both the iOS and Android operating systems. This app is a great resource—it quickly provides you with information regarding the FODMAP content of hundreds of food items. The app is continually being updated, so you can be assured that you are getting optimal research-based information.

Most people who try the low-FODMAP diet see significant improvement in their symptoms by the four-week mark, but you may find that you feel better even sooner. However, don't despair if it takes longer for you to see improvement—everyone's body is unique and will be affected differently by the diet.

How Long Should Your Elimination Phase Be?

FODMAP researchers recommend you remove high-FODMAP foods from your diet for four to eight weeks. In theory, the longer you can adhere to the Elimination Phase, the better. That being said, you can make the decision with the help of your physician or your nutritionist. It will also depend on how you are feeling and how quickly your body responds to the absence of problem foods. If you are feeling significantly better two weeks into the

Elimination Phase, you might be able to start the Challenge Phase after three weeks.

Restricted Foods

Foods that contain high levels of FODMAPS are not allowed at all during the Elimination Phase of the diet. However, if you've already undergone breath testing (see Chapter 1 and Chapter 2) and know that you don't have a problem with lactose, fructose, and/or polyols, you can include these tolerated foods right from the start.

Remember, the Elimination Phase is temporary. Although you will be avoiding foods on the restricted list for now, that does not necessarily mean you will never be able to enjoy them again. In the Challenge Phase of the diet you'll reintroduce foods and test your personal sensitivities. It's likely that you'll be able to add many of the restricted foods to your diet. Also, as you move beyond the Challenge Phase you may find that you can tolerate small amounts of a particular restricted food if you keep your overall intake of FODMAPs low for the rest of the day. Some people actually find that after following a low-FODMAP diet for a period of time, they increase their ability to tolerate previously troublesome foods.

Foods to Avoid (High-FODMAP Foods)

Let's take a look at the foods you will need to avoid during the Elimination Phase:

CONDIMENTS
- Barbecue sauce
- Gluten-containing soy sauce
- Worcestershire sauce
- Yellow mustard

DAIRY FOODS
- Buttermilk
- Cream
- Custard

- Ice cream
- Margarine
- Milk (cow, goat, and sheep)
- Soft cheese, including cream cheese, mascarpone, and ricotta
- Yogurt, regular and Greek

DAIRY SUBSTITUTES
- Almond milk
- Soy milk

BEVERAGES
- Rum
- Soda that contains high fructose corn syrup, sucralose, or any other high-FODMAP ingredient
- Sports drinks
- Teas: Chai (strongly brewed), chamomile, fennel, fruit-based herbal tea with chicory root, and oolong

FOOD ADDITIVES
- FOS (Fructooligosaccharides)
- Inulin (chicory root extract)
- Oligofructose (a form of inulin)

FRUITS
- Apple cider vinegar
- Apples
- Apricots
- Blackberries
- Canned fruits
- Cherries
- Dried fruits, with the exception of a small amount (1 tablespoon per serving) of cranberries
- Grapefruit
- Lychee
- Mango
- Most fruit juices

- Nectarines
- Peaches
- Pears
- Persimmon
- Plums and prunes
- Watermelon

GRAINS
- Barley
- Bulgur
- Couscous
- Farro
- Rye
- Semolina
- Wheat

LEGUMES
- Baked beans
- Black-eyed peas
- Butter beans
- Kidney beans
- Lima beans
- Soybeans
- Split peas

NUTS
- Cashews
- Pistachios

SWEETENERS
- Agave
- Fructose
- High fructose corn syrup (HFCS)
- Honey
- Inulin
- Isomalt

- Maltitol
- Mannitol
- Sorbitol
- Xylitol

VEGETABLES
- Artichokes
- Asparagus
- Beets
- Brussels sprouts (2 sprouts are allowed per serving)
- Cauliflower
- Celery
- Chicory
- Dandelion
- Garlic
- Leeks
- Mushrooms
- Onions
- Savoy cabbage
- Scallions (white parts)
- Shallots
- Snow peas
- Sugar snap peas

Allowed Foods (Low-FODMAP Foods)

After seeing all the foods on the restricted list you may be left wondering, "What *can* I eat?" But don't worry—you'll find a wide variety of delicious and nutritious foods on the approved lists. These foods can be included in your diet right from the start and through all phases of the diet. Of course, there is no guarantee that you will be able to tolerate them all. If you suspect that an "allowed" food is problematic for you, try avoiding that food during the Elimination Phase of the diet. You can test the problematic food during the Challenge Phase of your diet:

ALERT

Most of the research regarding the FODMAP content of food has come from the work of researchers in Australia. However, food preparation and growing conditions may be quite different in other parts of the world. This may explain why you might have a reaction to a food on the Allowed Foods list.

CONDIMENTS
- Brown mustard
- Dijon mustard
- Tamari (gluten-free only)

DAIRY PRODUCTS
- Butter
- Gelato
- Cheeses, including Brie, Camembert, Cheddar, Colby, cottage, feta, fontina, Havarti, mozzarella, Parmesan, pecorino, Swiss, and any hard variety
- Lactose-free products, such as lactose-free ice cream, milk, and yogurt
- Sorbet
- Sour cream (light)
- Whipped cream

DAIRY SUBSTITUTES
- Coconut milk
- Oat milk
- Rice milk

BEVERAGES
- Beer (limit 1 per serving)
- Coffee (limit to 1 cup per serving)
- Cranberry juice (limit to 1 cup per serving)
- Gin

- Teas: Black tea (weak), Chai tea (weak), green tea, fruit-based herbal tea with chicory root (weak), peppermint tea, white tea
- Vodka
- Whiskey
- Wine: red, sparkling, white

FRUITS
- Bananas
- Blueberries
- Boysenberries
- Cantaloupe
- Clementines
- Cranberries
- Dragon fruit
- Durian
- Grapes
- Honeydew melon
- Kiwi
- Lemons
- Limes
- Mandarin oranges
- Olives
- Oranges
- Papaya
- Passionfruit
- Pineapple
- Pomegranates (¼ cup seeds or ½ small fruit per serving)
- Prickly pears
- Raspberries
- Rhubarb
- Star fruit
- Strawberries
- Tangelos

GRAINS
- Amaranth
- Arrowroot

- Buckwheat
- Cornmeal
- Cornstarch
- Oats
- Millet
- Polenta
- Quinoa
- Rice
- Sourdough (gluten-free or artisanal)
- Spelt products (caution: these contain gluten)

HERBS AND SPICES
- Allspice
- Basil
- Cayenne
- Celery seed
- Chives
- Cilantro
- Cinnamon
- Coriander
- Crushed red pepper
- Cumin
- Dill
- Five spice powder
- Ginger
- Marjoram
- Mint
- Mustard seed
- Nutmeg
- Oregano
- Paprika
- Parsley
- Poppy seed
- Rosemary
- Tarragon
- Thyme
- Turmeric

LEGUMES

- Canned chickpeas, well rinsed (¼ cup serving)
- Canned lentils, well rinsed (½ cup serving)

TASTE ENHANCERS

- Almond extract
- Peppermint extract
- Vanilla extract
- Lemon juice
- Lime juice

NUTS AND SEEDS

- Almonds (limit 10 per serving)
- Brazil nuts
- Caraway seeds
- Chia seeds
- Hazelnuts (limit 10 per serving)
- Macadamia nuts
- Peanuts
- Pecans
- Pine nuts
- Pumpkin seeds
- Sesame seeds
- Sunflower seeds
- Walnuts
- Nut butters, except cashew butter

ANIMAL FOODS

- Beef
- Chicken
- Eggs
- Fish and shellfish
- Lamb
- Pork
- Turkey

ALTERNATIVE PROTEIN SOURCES

- Seitan (this is not gluten-free)
- Tempeh
- Tofu

SNACKS

- Gluten-free pretzels
- Potato chips
- Rice cakes, plain
- Sorbet

SWEETENERS

- Artificial sweeteners that do not end in −ol (aspartame, saccharine, sucralose)
- Glucose
- Maple syrup, pure, no high fructose corn syrup (HFCS)
- Molasses, blackstrap (1 tablespoon limit per serving)
- Powdered sugar
- Sugar, including brown sugar

VEGETABLES

- Alfalfa
- Arugula (rocket lettuce)
- Avocado (⅛ of whole per serving)
- Bamboo shoots
- Bell peppers
- Bok choy
- Broccoli (½ cup limit per serving)
- Butternut squash (limit to ¼ cup diced or less per serving)
- Carrots
- Celeriac
- Chili, red
- Chives
- Common (green) cabbage
- Cucumber
- Eggplant

- Endive
- Fennel (bulb, ½ cup limit per serving)
- Ginger
- Green beans
- Kale
- Lettuce (butter, red coral)
- Okra
- Parsley
- Parsnips
- Peas (¼ cup limit)
- Potatoes
- Pumpkin
- Radicchio (3 leaves limit per serving)
- Scallions (green parts only)
- Seaweed
- Snow peas (limit to 5 pods per serving)
- Spinach, baby
- Squash
- Sweet corn (limit ½ cob per serving)
- Sweet potatoes (½ cup serving or less)
- Tomatoes
- Turnips
- Water chestnuts
- Zucchini

VINEGARS
- Balsamic vinegar (limit to 1 tablespoon per serving)
- Red wine vinegar
- Rice wine vinegar
- White wine vinegar

MISCELLANEOUS FOODS AND INGREDIENTS
- Coconut, shredded (no more than ¼ cup per serving)
- Dried cranberries (limit 1 tablespoon per serving)
- Psyllium husk
- Rice sticks

- Rice wraps
- Sun-dried tomatoes (limit 2 per serving)

Use your best judgment regarding any foods that don't appear on these lists or the Monash University app. If you're not sure about a particular food, err on the side of caution and avoid the food during the Elimination Phase. You can then test your own sensitivity to the food when you get to the Challenge Phase.

Get Your Pantry Ready

Now that you know which foods are on the restricted list, it's time for a kitchen clean-out. This will require a time commitment, as you'll have to carefully read labels to find high-FODMAP ingredients. Give away, throw out, or freeze any high-FODMAP foods that are perishable and pack away the rest for the Challenge Phase of the diet.

ALERT

You may choose to keep restricted foods around in small amounts for the other members of your household, but do so only if you have faith that you will have the willpower necessary to avoid eating them! If the temptation seems too great, it's not worth sacrificing your digestive well-being!

All of the following should be temporarily removed from your kitchen:

- Restricted dairy foods
- Restricted beverages
- Any gluten-containing baked goods, cereal, and pasta
- Processed foods and condiments containing restricted ingredients, including artificial sweeteners
- Legumes, excluding chickpeas and lentils
- High-FODMAP fruits
- High-FODMAP vegetables

If you are the main cook in your family, prepare foods in a way that is suitable for the low-FODMAP diet. That includes making dishes that are gluten- and lactose-free. If you prepare a wide variety of FODMAP-friendly vegetables, fruits, and whole grains, everyone's nutritional needs should be accounted for. Consulting a dietitian can be very helpful for ensuring that you are covering all of the nutritional bases.

Food Shopping

As you adjust to the changes that the diet requires, food shopping may take a little longer than usual. It is important to take this into account as you plan your days and weeks. You will be at high risk for veering off of the diet if you don't have the time to properly assess the foods that you will be eating.

Label Reading

Carefully read the labels of all food you're considering buying. If you are unsure of an ingredient, place it back on the shelf until you can double-check that it is FODMAP-approved. If you are able to download the Monash app to your mobile device, you will find that it is a huge help in terms of giving you quick feedback so you can choose wisely.

Buy Whole Foods

Food manufacturers have a vested interest in including food additives, preservatives, artificial sweeteners, and other ingredients designed to lengthen shelf life and please the palate. The sad reality is that most manufacturers are focused on making profits and therefore are not focused on your health. The safest way to be assured that you are not consuming the ingredients your body is sensitive to is to minimize the amount of processed foods that you buy.

Whole foods are foods that are as close to their natural state as possible. A good rule of thumb is to ask yourself if your great-great-grandmother would recognize the food that you're buying. Whole foods are more likely to be found in the perimeter of the store. Another good rule of thumb is to only purchase foods that have a minimum number of ingredients (FODMAP-friendly, of course!). As the number of ingredients rise, so does the likelihood of poorly tolerated additives.

Take Advantage of Current Options

Food manufacturers have taken note of the rising number of people who have celiac disease, food allergies, and other types of food sensitivities. As a result you'll find that gluten-free and lactose-free food items are now more readily available. This makes it so much easier to successfully follow a low-FODMAP diet.

Beware of Calories

Just because a food is labeled "gluten-free" or "lactose-free" doesn't necessarily mean that it is healthy. In fact, sometimes these products are higher in calories, sugar, and food additives than their traditional counterparts. This is because food manufacturers use these added ingredients to try to mimic the flavor of "regular" foods. Read labels carefully so you can choose wisely.

Tips for Elimination Phase Success

The Elimination Phase is the most difficult phase of the diet. You are learning a whole new way of eating and the diet is, for now, at its most restrictive. Rest assured that the diet will get easier! In the meantime, here are some strategies that you can use to get through this phase.

Keep Up Your Symptom Diary

Continue to keep a record of what foods you eat and what symptoms you experience. If your symptoms are bad, the Symptom Diary will serve to remind you why you have undertaken this endeavor. If your symptoms are improving, you will have concrete evidence that the diet is working and that the drastic change was worth it.

Learn to Love Home Cooking

You maximize your ability to be successful on this diet if you are the one doing the cooking! Give yourself enough time to enjoy the pleasure of cooking real, whole foods for yourself and your family. This may mean that you have to change your schedule around a bit, but a slower pace of life is only going to help enhance your digestive health.

ESSENTIAL

Make cooking fun! Feel a sense of gratitude for the variety and abundance of the food you are preparing. Light a candle, put on some great music, and feel free to dance around your kitchen. Enlist other family members to help out, cutting down your workload and (hopefully!) adding to the fun factor.

You may want to make a list of your favorite foods and then set yourself the challenge of finding low-FODMAP substitutions. Similarly, you can pull out your favorite recipes and use your creativity to come up with a low-FODMAP version of each one. The recipes in this book will help support you and inspire you in this process.

Plan Out Your Meals

Make sure you have access to suitable foods at all times. This means paying attention to when you will need to take foods on the go. You don't want to find yourself in a position where there is nothing else to eat but foods that are high in FODMAPs! Planning your meals ahead of time means that you will never go hungry, never be tempted to stray from the diet, and still get in all your essential nutrients.

ESSENTIAL

There is no need to feel hungry on the low-FODMAP diet! Remember, this is not a weight loss diet. You are to restrict certain foods, but not restrict calories. If you are hungry, feel free to eat any foods on the allowed lists.

It is probably best to organize your meals both weekly and daily. At the beginning of the week, sit down and make an outline of the foods you will be eating during the next seven days. Plan out your breakfasts, lunches, dinners, and snacks. Be sure to have a variety of options available to provide for some flexibility. Use your weekly meal plan to create your grocery list—and stick to it. If you find that you are really struggling with food planning, it might be time to call in a dietitian or health coach.

In order to maximize adherence to the diet during the Elimination Phase, you should eat at home as much as possible.

It's helpful to also make a daily plan. You can write it down or just have it in your head, but in either case your daily plan will become the menu that you follow as you go through your day. This daily plan can be devised the night before or in the morning. It should take into account what your agenda and to-do list look like for that particular day.

Dealing with Emotions

As you make this major change to the way that you are eating, you are bound to experience some reactive emotions. This is perfectly normal! Hopefully, relief and gratitude will come up once you start to experience symptom improvement. However, other not-so-pleasant emotions may arise.

Frustration and Disappointment

IBS is an extremely frustrating disorder. Most people who have IBS have tried a wide variety of treatments and remedies only to be let down again and again when those things don't work or when symptoms return after a period of remission. Your body's response to the initial phase of the diet might also be somewhat up and down—with some symptom relief followed by a return of painful or disruptive symptoms. This unpredictability is normal as your body slowly begins to adjust to the dietary changes that you're making.

Anxiety

Many IBS patients bristle when told that their IBS is caused by stress, not just because this is a misguided notion, but because for them it is the IBS that is the main source of stress! With a body that is unpredictable and can react to foods violently, it is understandable that you will be quite anxious about the foods you are eating or about any perceived symptom within your body. The problem is that anxiety, due to the brain-gut connection, can further exacerbate digestive symptoms.

Self-Pity

It is completely understandable if you are having some "Why me?" thoughts as you undertake this new way of eating. "Why can't I eat like normal people?" may be going through your head. Allow yourself a little self-empathy and recognize that it is okay to grieve the loss of the freedom to eat whatever you want.

ESSENTIAL

Slowing down your breathing can have a relaxing effect on the body and help to turn off the stress response that is triggered by anxiety. The nice thing about deep-breathing techniques is that you can practice them any time, any place. Practice taking deep, long breaths, concentrating on the movement of your abdomen as you breathe in and out.

On the other hand, not eating like a "normal" person is not necessarily a bad thing! The standard Western diet is not a healthy one, as evidenced by rising rates of obesity, heart disease, diabetes, and cancer. Following a diet that is tailored to your specific health needs allows for the possibility of an improvement to your overall health. That is, of course, if you choose to eat lots of FODMAP-friendly vegetables, fruits, and whole grains, get your protein in, and minimize your intake of processed foods with all of their additives.

Once you have acknowledged the validity of your "self-pity," you can reframe the diet as a strategy for some well-deserved self-care. It hasn't been easy dealing with your IBS. You are now taking active steps to significantly reduce the negative impact that IBS has had on your life. You will be enjoying a heightened focus on the health of the foods you are eating, in sharp contrast to the heightened sense of fear you may have experienced before starting the diet. This heightened awareness of healthy foods—foods that make your digestive system happy—will have health benefits that go beyond addressing your IBS.

Dietary Slips

Everyone makes mistakes. Even with your best efforts to adhere to the diet, you may slip once in a while. That, however, is not a major cause for alarm.

You may pay for your slip in terms of increased digestive symptoms, but that can serve to keep you motivated to make the changes you need to make. A temporary setback will not do any permanent damage to your health.

It is important to take slips in stride. When it comes to weight-loss diets, people have the tendency to give up on diets altogether after a single "cheat." The low-FODMAP diet is a very different type of diet. Slipping here and there does not mean that you will not experience the benefits of the diet and therefore should just give up. Accounting for the notion of "FODMAP load," you may be able to ingest some high-FODMAP foods without becoming symptomatic.

ALERT

Research has shown consistently that the better the adherence to the diet, the better the treatment outcome. Therefore, don't let your "slips" become habits. You may get away with cheating with a specific food one day and then pay for it royally on another because of other foods that you have eaten.

If you have a slip, use it as a learning opportunity. Did you eat something without knowing fully what its FODMAP level was? Did you find yourself in a situation where you felt you had no other food options? Did you succumb to peer pressure? Analyzing what went wrong can help you to figure out strategies to make a better food choice the next time around. Record these thoughts in your Symptom Diary.

CHAPTER 4

The Challenge Phase

Congratulations on making it through the Elimination Phase of the diet! Most likely, you are feeling significantly better. In this next phase, you will be reintroducing your body to the foods that you love. You will do this by working your way through the various FODMAP types, group by group. You will gain a better awareness of which foods contain which FODMAPs and which foods your body is able to tolerate. In doing so, you will now be able to eat more of your favorite foods with confidence.

Food Reintroduction

The first step of the Challenge Phase is to start to reintroduce foods back into your diet. You may have mixed emotions about this. On the one hand, you may be excited to try some of your old favorites. On the other hand, you may be very anxious that the foods you will now be eating are going to make you feel lousy again.

ALERT

Please don't be tempted to view the low-FODMAP diet as a long-term solution. Many high-FODMAP foods provide important health benefits. This includes substances known as prebiotics, which are essential for the health of your gut flora. In addition, fermentation of FODMAPs produces short-chain fatty acids that may protect against cancer. Last, the laxative effect of FODMAPs helps to prevent constipation.

If you are feeling reluctant, keep in mind that the process of challenging yourself with higher-FODMAPs food is an essential part of the diet. It is crucial that you expand the range of foods you are eating to ensure you are covering all of your nutritional bases. Although eating a new food might cause you to experience some of those old, awful digestive symptoms, at least you will know why and no longer feel that your body is unpredictable and out of control. It really is best to consult with a qualified dietary professional to help you through this process.

Planning for the Challenge Phase

You will be introducing foods into your diet one FODMAP group at a time. Before you begin, you will need to figure out the order you would like to follow. You will spend approximately one week on each FODMAP type.

As you make out your shopping lists, keep in mind that you will be remaining on the diet you followed in the Elimination Phase throughout the whole Challenge Phase. The only exception will be the food that you pick for your FODMAP challenge each week. Don't buy too much of any perishable item, as your consumption of these foods will be fairly minimal and only for a one-week period.

Order of Reintroduction

You can decide which order you would like to follow as you challenge yourself with each type of FODMAP. Your starting options include fructose, lactose, or polyols (sorbitol and mannitol). Fructans and GOS should be saved for last, as they are not absorbed by anyone. They are an important part of the diet, so don't be tempted to pass them by altogether!

Step-by-Step Guide to Reintroduction

The following steps can be used as a general guideline for the challenge process:

1. On Monday, eat a small amount of food containing the FODMAP you are testing.
2. On Tuesday, if you experienced no severe reaction to Monday's trial, you can eat the food again, but this time in a portion size that is typical for you.
3. On Wednesday, eat only the foods you have been eating throughout the Elimination Phase.
4. On Thursday, if you continue to experience no severe symptoms, eat the challenge food in the same portion two or three more times in the day.
5. Friday through Sunday, go back to your Elimination Phase diet.
6. The following Monday, start over again with a food from the next FODMAP group.

If You Have No Symptoms

If you do not experience a return of your digestive symptoms after introducing a new food, you can conclude that your body can tolerate that food and other foods from that FODMAP group. Make note of this in your Symptom Diary. Sadly, you will have to put these foods aside temporarily until you have gone through all of the FODMAP groups, but they will be waiting for you when you get to the other side! The reason you cannot eat them freely now is that you don't want "FODMAP load" to complicate the picture as you assess the effect of each FODMAP group still to be tested.

If Your Symptoms Return

If your symptoms return in response to a reintroduced food, go back to your Elimination Phase food until you feel better. If you experience a severe reaction to the small Monday dose, it is okay to conclude that you have a sensitivity to this FODMAP. It would be a good idea to try this food again in the future to see if your tolerance has improved.

ESSENTIAL

A FODMAP can be identified as problematic if your food challenge results in abdominal pain, bloating, constipation, diarrhea, or excessive gas. Remember that intestinal gas is a normal part of digestion, as it is a byproduct of fermentation of FODMAPs by gut bacteria—a process that is essential for your overall health. Do not declare a sensitivity to a food just because you experience moderate amounts of gas.

If you experienced moderate to severe symptoms in response to your regular portion size, wait until all symptoms subside and then retest the food, starting with the small dose on Monday, but then half of your original portion size on Tuesday. Although this may seem like the last thing you want to do, it is the only way to figure out your body's tolerance level for each FODMAP. Another option is to try a different food from the same FODMAP group, starting on a Monday, to help you to come to a more definitive conclusion regarding a confirmed sensitivity.

Tips for Challenge Phase Success

The goal of the Challenge Phase is that you get a good sense of which FODMAPs are right for you and which FODMAPs you should continue to restrict. Proper planning, an inquisitive mind, and a flexible attitude will help you to best achieve this goal.

Choosing Challenge Foods

As you decide which food to try for each FODMAP challenge, you may as well pick the foods you like best. Other than the small portion size on a

Monday, don't worry about measuring out portions, as you need this way of eating to be as easy as it can be. Therefore, it is okay to eat a food at your regular portion size.

Be sure to pick a food that contains only one type of FODMAP. The food lists that appear later in this chapter will help you with this. Remember that you are trying to be as scientific as possible in order to accurately pinpoint which FODMAP types are more tolerable and which types give you more trouble.

ESSENTIAL

Don't forget about the notion of "FODMAP load." This refers to the fact that the higher the amount of FODMAPs in your system, the more likely you are to have symptoms, regardless of FODMAP type or your personal sensitivities. Therefore, don't pile it on! Eat a reasonable amount of each food. You are looking to find the amounts of each FODMAP your body can tolerate.

If you are truly undecided about where to start, it may be helpful to know which foods FODMAP researchers recommend:

- Fructose challenge: Honey
- Lactose challenge: Regular milk
- Mannitol challenge: Mushrooms
- Sorbitol challenge: Blackberries

Don't Skip the Fructan and GOS Challenges

You should end the Challenge Phase with a trial of fructans and GOS. Although foods with these FODMAPs are gas producing for everyone, there are reasons to include them in your diet at the amount you can tolerate. Foods containing ingredients from these groups are extremely common. Therefore, it will be easier for you to find things to eat if you know how much of these FODMAPs you can tolerate. Also, these foods are thought to be very beneficial to the health of your gut flora. At the very least, the hope is that you will be able to tolerate small amounts of garlic and small servings of legumes as you proceed beyond the Elimination and Challenge Phases of the diet.

Keep Up Your Symptom Diary

Your Symptom Diary is going to be your best friend through this process. Keep careful track of what foods you eat when and in what portion size. Continue to record any symptoms. Don't forget about other circumstances that can affect digestion. Recording these will help you to decide if symptoms are truly due to the challenged FODMAP or if some other factor is at play. Remember, FODMAPs are not the only things that cause digestive distress. Your Symptom Diary may reveal some clues to these other factors. For example, eating too much junk food, being under inordinate stress, or being hit with a virus could all cause symptoms separate from your intake of the challenged FODMAP.

Planning Around Your Life

Forgive the redundancy, but the Challenge Phase can be a challenge. There is a chance that you will re-experience those awful IBS symptoms that prompted you to try this diet in the first place. Therefore, it is not only okay, but advisable, to embark on a new FODMAP group on a day when you know you have no major commitments lined up for that week. This will help you to weather a new storm of symptoms without too much wear and tear on your life.

Don't Be Tempted to Cheat

You have come this far in terms of sticking to the restricted diet of the Elimination Phase. You only have a few more weeks to go before you can begin to eat as normal a diet as you can. It is important for you to continue to eat only allowed foods, with the exception of the challenge foods, so you can gain accurate information about your own personal sensitivities.

Although it may be tempting to continue eating a reintroduced food that you had no reactivity to, this will muddy up the results of the food being tested due to FODMAP load. Therefore it is important to eat only low-FODMAP foods while each new food is being tested. If however, you have been eating foods approved after a hydrogen breath test (HBT) all along, you may continue to enjoy those foods. (See Hydrogen Breath Testing in Chapter 1.)

If you do have a slip that results in symptoms, return to your Elimination Phase diet until you feel better. You will need to start over with whatever FODMAP was being challenged during the week of your slip so as to gain accurate information about your sensitivity to that particular FODMAP.

Foods Containing Fructose

The following foods contain high levels of fructose and thus are appropriate for a fructose challenge. Although many fruits contain fructose, they often have other FODMAPs as well, so these are not included on the following list. Such fruits can be reintroduced after you have challenged all five FODMAP groups.

Fructose-Containing Beverages

- Orange juice
- Rum

Fructose-Containing Fruits

Cherries, when limited to three, contain high amounts of fructose. Six cherries would increase the level of sorbitol to a moderately high level. Other fruits may contain fructose, but also contain other FODMAPs.

Fructose-Containing Vegetables

The following vegetables would be appropriate for a fructose challenge:

- Artichoke, globe or hearts
- Asparagus
- Sugar snap peas
- Sun-dried tomatoes (4 pieces per serving; 2 pieces are considered low-FODMAP)

Fructose-Containing Sweeteners

- Agave nectar
- High fructose corn syrup (HFCS)
- Honey

Foods Containing Lactose

The following foods all contain lactose. This list has been split into two levels: The first set of foods have levels of lactose that are only moderately high—you may find that you can tolerate these foods, even if you have difficulty with those on the list of foods with higher lactose levels. Lactose is the exception to the rule regarding paying close attention to portion size; you may be able to expand your dietary choices significantly if you can tolerate foods on the moderate list.

Foods with Moderately High Levels of Lactose

- Cream (½ cup serving)
- Cream cheese (¼ cup serving)
- Ricotta cheese (¼ cup serving)
- Sour cream (½ cup serving)

Foods with Higher Levels of Lactose

- Buttermilk
- Custard
- Ice cream
- Milk
- Yogurt

Foods Containing Polyols

The Monash University researchers have broken the polyol category into foods containing mannitol and those containing sorbitol.

Mannitol-Containing Vegetables

- Mushrooms (½ cup limit per serving)
- Cauliflower
- Celery
- Sweet potato (more than ½ cup per serving)

Sorbitol-Containing Fruits

- Avocado (serving size ¼ fruit or more)
- Blackberries
- Peaches, clingstone or yellow
- Prunes (limit to 2 per serving, or fructan level will rise)

ALERT

Foods containing artificial sweeteners are likely to contain sorbitol. Look for ingredients ending in "-ol" on recipe labels. Aspartame and saccharine do not contain sorbitol, but this does not mean they are necessarily good for your health! Satisfy your sweet tooth with small amounts of foods made with real sugar.

Foods Containing Fructans

The foods on these next few lists, as well as anything with chicory root or inulin, contain fructans.

Fructan-Containing Fruits

- Dates, dried
- Figs, dried
- Grapefruit
- Persimmon
- Pomegranate, ½ cup seeds or 1 small fruit (¼ cup seeds or ½ small fruit is low-FODMAP)
- Raisins

Fructan-Containing Grains

All wheat, rye, or barley-based products contain high levels of fructans, so you can challenge fructans with any gluten-containing versions of the following foods. Do not eat any of these foods if you have celiac disease:

- Baked goods
- Bread
- Cereal
- Couscous
- Pasta
- Pretzels
- Pizza dough

Fructan-Containing Vegetables

- Artichokes
- Beets
- Garlic
- Leeks
- Onions, yellow and red
- Savoy (curly) cabbage
- Scallions (white part)
- Shallots

Foods Containing GOS

The following foods contain high levels of GOS:

- Almonds (20 nuts)
- Lima beans
- Cannellini beans
- Green peas (½ cup or more; ¼ cup is low-FODMAP)
- Soy milk

Foods with Multiple FODMAPs

The following foods contain high levels of more than one type of FODMAP. Thus, they are not appropriate for your initial reintroductions. Once you have challenged each of the five FODMAP groups and have a better sense of which types of FODMAPs you can and cannot handle, you can try these foods to see how your body tolerates them. These lists are useful for restriction purposes for anyone who is trying the One-by-One approach.

Fructan and Fructose

Jerusalem artichoke is one of the few foods that contain high levels of both fructans and fructose, but without any additional FODMAPs.

Fructan and GOS

- Split peas
- Chickpeas (not canned; ¼ cup canned per serving is low-FODMAP)
- Lentils (not canned; ½ cup canned per serving is low-FODMAP)
- Black beans
- Butter beans
- Navy beans
- Red kidney beans

Fructan and Mannitol

Fennel, at higher than a half-cup serving, contains both fructan and mannitol; a half-cup serving is considered low-FODMAP.

Fructan and Sorbitol

- Apricots
- Nectarines

Fructose and Sorbitol

- Apple, Granny Smith
- Apple juice
- Cherries (6 or more per serving)
- Pears

Fructan, Fructose, and GOS

- Baked beans
- Lima beans

Fructan, Fructose, and Mannitol

Watermelon contains these three FODMAPs in combination.

Fructan, GOS, and Sorbitol

Brussels sprouts in a serving of more than six sprouts contain these three FODMAPs in combination. A serving size of two sprouts is allowed in all phases of the diet.

Fructan, GOS, and Mannitol

Snow peas contain all three of these FODMAPs. A serving size of five snow pea pods is allowed in all phases of the diet.

GOS and Fructan

- Cashews
- Hazelnuts (10 or more per serving)
- Pistachios

GOS and Mannitol

Butternut squash contains both of these FODMAPs, although a quarter-cup serving is considered low-FODMAP and is allowed on all phases of the diet.

GOS and Sorbitol

Sweet corn contains these two FODMAPs, although you should be able to tolerate one-half of a cob in all phases of the diet.

Ending the Challenge Phase

Once you have challenged all five FODMAP groups, you can be assured that the hardest parts of the diet are now behind you. You have given your body time to heal, and you have systematically evaluated your body's response to each FODMAP. Now you can increase your daily food choices by slowly incorporating the FODMAPs-containing foods that passed your challenges.

QUESTION

What if I can't handle any FODMAPs?
If you are not able to tolerate any FODMAPs, it is best to consult with a qualified dietary professional. The low-FODMAP diet at its strictest was only designed for short-term use. Working with a dietitian or health coach can help to ensure that you are getting adequate nutrition. You should also continue to rechallenge each FODMAP group at scheduled times in the future.

The One-by-One Approach

In this approach, you will be restricting all foods from a selected FODMAP group for a period of one week and assessing how your body responds to the restriction. This approach is not as scientific as getting through the full Elimination Phase followed by the systematic reintroductions of the Challenge Phase. It does, however, provide for more flexibility in terms of what you can and cannot eat on any given day. After you have gone through a period of restriction of each specific FODMAP type, you should gain some valuable information regarding your body's tolerance levels.

Foods to Restrict

You can make use of the lists provided in the earlier sections of this chapter to help guide you in your food restriction choices. However, keep in mind that these lists are quite limited, as they only contain foods that have been tested by Monash University for their FODMAP content (at the time of this writing). Many other foods contain the FODMAP ingredients you will need to avoid. When in doubt, err on the side of caution, and restrict. You can make educated guesses based on foods that are similar. For example, restrict all beans on a GOS challenge, or fruits that do not show up on the allowed list in this chapter for a fructose challenge.

You can choose from any of the five groups to start. There may be an advantage to starting with either fructans or GOS, due to the fact that they are malabsorbed by all. This might give you some more immediate relief and keep you motivated to keep going with this whole complicated process!

Alternatively, you could start with the FODMAP group that you know you tend to eat most frequently.

ALERT

If you are trying the One-by-One approach, be sure to look at the lists of foods that contain more than one identified FODMAP. You will need to restrict any foods from those lists (as well as foods that seem similar to them) that contain the FODMAP you are currently avoiding.

Step-by-Step Guide to One-by-One Approach

The following steps can be used as a general guide through this process. Slips that occur when using this approach are not a big deal; just start your one-week restriction all over again.

1. Pick one FODMAP group to avoid, e.g., fructans, fructose, GOS, lactose, mannitol, or sorbitol.
2. Avoid all foods that contain ingredients from that FODMAP type for a period of one week.
3. If symptoms improve after the one-week restriction, go back to eating foods from that group for at least three days and assess your symptoms. If symptoms don't improve after the one-week restriction, mark the FODMAP as questionable and add it back to your regular diet.
4. Start a new week with a restriction of a new FODMAP group.

Symptom Improvement after Restriction

If you see symptom improvement after restricting a particular FODMAP group, and your symptoms return after the three-day reintroduction, you may have identified a FODMAP that you don't tolerate well. You can mark this as a problematic FODMAP for you and go back to restricting foods from this group from your diet. If you feel great with this or any one restriction, there is no need to continue the process of challenging other FODMAPs.

If you are still experiencing some symptoms even with the restriction of any FODMAP that you marked as problematic, you can continue to restrict it and make your way through all of the FODMAP groups until you either feel completely well or have completed a challenge on each FODMAP. This process should give you some valuable information regarding your body's sensitivity to each of the FODMAP groups.

No Improvement after Restriction

If at the end of the one-week period you don't see any symptom improvement, mark the restricted FODMAP as questionable and add its foods back to your diet in preparation to move on to the next FODMAP group. The reason for adding the food back is that you cannot yet make a determination regarding your sensitivity to foods from that group. You can't conclude that this particular FODMAP is bad for you because you don't know if other FOD-MAPs might be causing you to continue to be symptomatic.

Once you have gone through all FODMAP groups, you can revisit any that are questionable. If you are feeling fine because you have identified and are restricting any FODMAPs that you are sensitive to, you can conclude that any of your questionable FODMAPs are okay for you. If you have experienced only mild to moderate relief from restricting other FODMAPs, you should do another one-week restriction of each questionable FODMAP, followed by a three-day challenge to see how your body reacts.

ESSENTIAL

Be sure to keep up your Symptom Diary throughout the One-by-One approach. Keep track of the foods you eliminate from your diet, and carefully note the effect each particular restriction and subsequent re-challenge is having on your symptoms.

Once you have worked through all the FODMAP groups, you should have a better sense of which foods you are sensitive to. Just as in the instructions for the full elimination diet, you should rechallenge foods down the road to reassess sensitivity. Remember, the goal is to be sure you eat the widest range of foods that you can tolerate and that you not restrict your food intake unnecessarily.

Rechallenging

A continual process of adding more foods into your diet is an essential part of the low-FODMAP diet. Whether you have chosen to undergo a full FOD-MAP elimination diet, the One-by-One approach, or the casual approach (see Chapter 2), you should make a schedule for regular rechallenges of the FODMAPs that you have identified as being problematic for you. Remember that with time, your ability to tolerate high-FODMAP foods may improve. You also may find that you are able to tolerate small portions of foods containing the FODMAPs you are reactive to. FODMAPs contain many health benefits and therefore play an essential role in a healthy diet. For that reason, you should try to get as many into your diet as you can tolerate.

Rechallenge Scheduling

There are no hard-and-fast rules when it comes to figuring out when the time is right for a FODMAP rechallenge. You might want to consider retesting at three-month intervals. Of course, you can be flexible with this process depending on how you have been feeling and what is going on in your life at the time. You may want to set a reminder in your day planner or on your mobile device. It is okay to be flexible with this process; just remember to keep striving to expand the range of foods that you feel comfortable eating. Follow the same steps for each rechallenge that you did in your original challenge.

If the Diet Doesn't Help

It can be so disheartening to have another IBS treatment fail to make a difference. Sadly, there is a small percentage of people for whom the diet doesn't work. If you didn't get the relief you were seeking though the diet, there still are a few things to consider.

Assess Your Adherence

Did you try only the One-by-One or casual approach to identify your FODMAP sensitivities? If so, it would be good to try the full Elimination Phase. If you did choose the Elimination Phase approach, were you able to fully restrict high-FODMAP foods from your diet, or did you have many slips? Remember that success with the diet is very much related to adherence.

Rule Out SIBO

If your symptoms are more likely to occur within ninety minutes of eating and you didn't get tested for SIBO prior to starting the diet, you may want to speak to your doctor about setting up a breath hydrogen test. Remember that you will need to eat foods high in FODMAPs in order to get an accurate result. If SIBO is present, your doctor may choose to treat you with a course of antibiotics.

Rule Out a Casein Allergy

Casein is a protein found in milk and therefore dairy products. The low-FODMAP diet allows for dairy products that are low in lactose or are lactose-free, but it is possible that you are reacting to the casein in these products. Try to restrict yourself from all dairy products for a period of two to four weeks and assess the effect of this restriction on your symptoms.

Cut Out Other Irritants

FODMAPs are not the only things that affect the functioning of your digestive system. Try to eliminate alcohol, caffeine, and foods that contain saturated and trans fats, such as fried food and fatty meats. You can also try to reduce meal size, as extra-large meals can result in stronger intestinal contractions.

Although some forms of sugar are allowed in the low-FODMAP diet, your system may not tolerate sugar of any form. As hard as it might be, try to eliminate added sugar from your diet, whether it be in the form of sweet treats or as hidden ingredients in other foods, to see if that helps to reduce your symptoms.

Try an Elimination Diet

A traditional elimination diet requires that for a period of two to eight weeks you avoid eating foods that are most likely to be a source of sensitivity. Elimination diets are thought to be effective in helping the gut to "heal," theoretically by correcting gut dysbiosis and reducing intestinal permeability.

The foods most typically recommended for restriction are:

- Coffee
- Corn
- Dairy
- Eggs
- Gluten
- Sugar
- Soy

You could also continue to eliminate high-FODMAP foods that are not on the previous list. Once you have followed the elimination diet for a period of time, you would follow a reintroduction process similar to that of the Challenge Phase of the low-FODMAP diet. One by one, slowly reintroduce each food group into your diet and assess your symptoms.

Get Support

A consultation with a dietitian or health coach may help to identify any factors contributing to your poor response to the diet. Alternatively, you may have more success with the diet if you have the support and accountability inherent in working with a dietary professional.

Be sure to find ways to connect with other individuals who understand what it is like to live with a chronic disorder. Online support groups provide a comfortable place to discuss the intimate details of digestive symptoms as well as to gain additional ideas in terms of treatments, dietary changes, resources, and over-the-counter remedies.

ESSENTIAL

Continue to stay in close contact with your physician. He or she is in the best position to monitor your symptoms over time and to make sure you have an accurate diagnosis. Your physician will also be a resource in terms of letting you know whenever new medications become available.

You may also want to consider trying a mind-body treatment such as cognitive-behavioral therapy (CBT) or hypnotherapy (see Chapter 2). Both forms of treatment have strong research support in terms of their effectiveness at reducing the symptoms of IBS. In addition, your therapist can help to support you as you face the challenges inherent in living a life with a chronic illness.

CHAPTER 5

Living Low-FODMAP

Most likely, you are living in a high-FODMAP world. Wheat, dairy, garlic, and onion can be found pretty much everywhere in Western cuisine. If you are a vegetarian or happen to adore Mexican food, beans are also a big part of your diet. Following a low-FODMAP diet is going to take some getting used to as you figure out how to manage socializing, dining out, and traveling. With planning, practice, and a body that feels much better, living low-FODMAP will become more doable.

Eating Out

The ability to eat out is a wonderful luxury. Food options are more varied and it is certainly nice to have someone else do the cooking. The downside of eating out is that you give up control as to what ingredients are in the foods you will be eating. If you are in the Elimination Phase, you may want to try to eat at home as much as possible. However, no matter what phase of the diet you are in, it is possible to enjoy the convenience of dining out. Although dining out low-FODMAP presents some challenges, you will find it to be a wonderful change of pace to have the confidence that you can enjoy the outing without worrying that your IBS will act up.

Pick a Good Place

As you lead your low-FODMAP life, you will need to do a little research to find out which restaurants will be most suitable for your new dietary needs. Some restaurants are very amenable to catering to individual needs, while others just naturally provide more low-FODMAP options. As a general rule, restaurants that have many gluten-free menu options would be more likely to accommodate your needs. Cuisines in which rice is a primary ingredient, e.g., Asian or Greek, may also provide you with more safe options. Over time, you will start to develop a new list of your favorite go-to restaurants.

ESSENTIAL

Many restaurants now publish their menus online. Take advantage of this option to figure out if a particular restaurant will be able to provide you with something you can safely eat. This also allows you to plan out your order without feeling pressured by the wait staff or the people you are dining with.

To set your mind at ease, you can call a restaurant ahead of time to alert the staff about your special dietary needs. Find out how flexible the kitchen is and what accommodations can be made. If you call before the restaurant opens for the day, the head chef may even be willing to speak with you about what the kitchen staff can cook especially for you.

Be Assertive!

Are you a person who doesn't like to make a fuss? It is time to flex your assertiveness muscles, because your health is on the line. You don't deserve to find yourself in pain and digestive distress after a meal just because you didn't want to be a bother. Remember, it is the aim of most dining establishments that their patrons leave happy.

Assertiveness is the art of asking for what you need in a way that is clear and direct without being aggressive. You can politely tell your server, "I am on a special diet for my stomach and I need to be sure that what I am ordering does not contain any wheat, garlic, or onions. Can you please tell me what ingredients are in this dish?" If you are with other people, and don't want to draw attention to yourself, quietly leave the table and pull the server or manager aside. If your needs cannot be accommodated, and the people you are with are flexible, it is perfectly acceptable to leave the restaurant and find a place where you can eat comfortably.

What to Order

Although most menu items will likely be off-limits, there are things that would be appropriate even for the Elimination Phase of the diet:

- Breakfast oatmeal (no milk or high-FODMAP toppings)
- Eggs, including omelets with low-FODMAP fillings
- Spinach or mixed green salad (remove high-FODMAP items such as onions); oil and vinegar dressing
- Grilled chicken, fish, steak, pork, or lamb, including onion-free kabobs
- Baked potato, sweet potato (½ cup per serving)
- Rice, white or brown
- Steamed low-FODMAP vegetables
- Gluten-free pizza, cheese only if sauce contains garlic or onions
- Gluten-free pasta with butter and low-FODMAP cheese
- Corn tortillas and chips
- Dessert: Sorbet, gelato, or low-FODMAP fruit

Fast-Food Restaurants

Fast-food restaurants do not typically have much in the way of food that is good for your digestive and overall health. If you have IBS, you already know how hard fast food can be on your body! Therefore, try to avoid fast-food joints whenever you can. However, there are times when they might be your only option.

ESSENTIAL

Most fast-food chains have nutritional fact sheets readily available for all of their menu items. Read them carefully to look for hidden high-FODMAP ingredients, such as wheat, dairy, and onion and garlic powders. If you are unsure of an ingredient, it is best to err on the side of caution.

Safe breakfast choices in fast-food restaurants are limited, but you may be able to find an egg item that is appropriate. As always, be sure to check ingredients first. For lunch and dinner, salad with grilled chicken is a good option. Some fast-food restaurants offer baked potatoes. Order them plain and treat yourself to a little butter. Read the ingredient list before ordering French fries or hash browns, as they may contain wheat and/or dairy. If the fast-food establishment offers gluten-free choices, be sure before you order that they don't contain any other high-FODMAP ingredients.

Parties and Other Social Engagements

If you are like many people with IBS, social invitations may have become a thing that causes dread. How can you commit to anything if you don't know if your IBS is going to act up? Luckily, the low-FODMAP diet can make that anticipatory anxiety a thing of the past. However, you may still find yourself with concerns about what you can safely eat when you are attending a social gathering. The difference now is that you can knowledgably choose what to eat and what to avoid, rather than grabbing something and hoping for the best.

Advance Planning

Please feel free to call ahead and discuss the diet with your host. If someone has invited you to their home it means they value your company and will want you to be comfortable. Explain that you are on this special diet and ask what they will be serving. Ask them if it is okay if you bring along a low-FODMAP side or main dish.

If you do not know your host or are very uncomfortable with calling ahead, you always have the option of making sure that you eat before you go so that you will not be hungry. This way you can be very choosy about what you eat and you will not be tempted to eat high-FODMAP foods and pay for your choices later.

What to Eat at Parties

You can follow the same guidelines for eating at parties that you will follow when eating at restaurants, although typically you may have fewer options. Because your main meal choices may be FODMAP-filled pasta dishes, meats in sauces, and gluten-containing subs, you may want to skip standard dietary advice and fill up on pre-dinner snack foods:

- Crudité platter: If you can tolerate raw vegetables, choose low-FODMAP ones and skip the dip
- Fresh low-FODMAP fruit
- Low-FODMAP cheese, such as Brie or Cheddar
- Popcorn
- Nuts (not cashew or pistachio; limit almonds and hazelnuts to 10 per serving)

What to Drink at Parties

Sometimes you are focusing so carefully on what you are eating that you can forget the importance of paying attention to what you are drinking. Soda may be out due to the presence of high fructose corn syrup (HFCS) or artificial sweeteners. It is also best to avoid fruit juices, with the notable exception of cranberry juice. Water always makes for a safe and healthy option.

As for alcohol, remember that separate from FODMAP levels, alcohol can be a gastrointestinal (GI) irritant. Monash researchers allow for one beer, but you will have to see for yourself if your system can handle that. Gin, vodka, and whiskey are all allowed, but it may be difficult to find low-FODMAP mixers. Your safest bet might be to limit yourself to one glass of red or white wine.

Traveling Low-FODMAP

One of the most challenging times for eating low-FODMAP, or eating healthy at all for that matter, is when you are traveling. Food choices are often extremely limited, as you have to rely on what is around you; often your only options are fast-food establishments. Because food choices can be limited, it may be best to not schedule any travel while you are in the Elimination Phase of the diet. If you do have to travel, you will need to spend time planning for what you will eat as you also consider what clothes to pack.

Low-FODMAP Road Trips

Traveling in your own car does make traveling low-FODMAP a little easier because you can pack your car and a cooler with plenty of low-FODMAP snacks and meal items. Crunchy Granola (see Chapter 6) and Chocolaty Trail Mix (see Chapter 15), as well as low-FODMAP raw vegetables, fruits, and cheeses are all extremely portable snacks. These snacks can serve double duty as meal substitutes if you are unable to find any FODMAP-friendly foods while on the road.

ESSENTIAL

On a typical road trip, most people tend to stop for food when they get hungry as opposed to planning to stop at any specific destination. Whenever possible, try to plan your meal stops at larger towns, where you may have more food choices. If you can't do that, use the suggestions mentioned earlier in this chapter for safely navigating through fast-food establishments.

Air Travel

Air travel poses its own set of challenges. Although packing your own low-FODMAP snacks is ideal, you may be limited by space or airline and security restrictions. Before your trip, be sure to check the latest regulations regarding what foods can be brought through security. In addition, you can call the airline ahead of time to see what accommodations are offered for people who have special dietary needs. Find out if the airline has any restrictions regarding foods (e.g., nuts) that are allowed on the airplane. Since air travel can present few food options, try to arrive at the airport with a full stomach.

The Low-FODMAP Diet and Your Wallet

Following the low-FODMAP diet doesn't have to break your budget. Although buying gluten-free items and fresh vegetables and fruits can be more expensive, you also will be eating more home-cooked meals, which may save you money. And don't forget how much you will be saving on OTC remedies and prescription copays! Here are some other ideas for frugal low-FODMAP living:

- Buy your low-FODMAP rice and grains in bulk. As these are perishable foods, be sure to store them safely.
- Make your own flours, stocks, and nut butters. Not only will you be saving money, but you will also have full control over included ingredients.
- Make your own breakfast cereals, baked treats, and snack items. You will find plenty of ideas in Chapters 6, 14, and 15.
- Plan out a weekly menu so as to avoid the more expensive option of takeout foods. Planning your meals ahead will also help with that all-important adherence to the diet.
- Make one night a week leftover night. Line up the week's leftovers on the counter like a cruise ship buffet and allow family members to pick and choose their favorites.
- Grow your own organic vegetables and fruits. You will save money, avoid pesticides and fertilizers, and get some soul-satisfying contact with Mother Nature—all through this one leisure activity.

The Low-FODMAP Diet and Your Weight

The low-FODMAP diet was not designed to be a weight loss diet. However, any change in the way that you eat has the potential for changing your weight. There are a few things you will want to keep in mind so that you can follow the low-FODMAP diet and either keep your weight stable or move it in the direction of a healthier weight.

Goal: Weight Loss

The low-FODMAP diet can absolutely be used as part of an overall weight loss program. You may lose some weight naturally, as you will be eating less unhealthy processed food, junk food, and fast food. If you pay close attention to your fiber needs, you will be giving your body more vegetables, fruits, and whole grains—all of which can help you to shed those unwanted pounds.

ALERT

Watch out for hidden, fattening ingredients in gluten-free processed foods. Many people mistakenly assume these foods are healthier, but actually they often are filled with unhealthy amounts of sugar, refined carbohydrates, and other additives to make them taste like their gluten-filled counterparts. Try to keep your consumption of these products to a minimum.

Trying to Gain Weight on a Low-FODMAP Diet

Although weight loss is not a symptom of IBS, some people with IBS lose weight due to an avoidance of food out of fear of triggering symptoms. If this has been your experience, you may find that you naturally put on weight with the low-FODMAP diet because you are able to eat with confidence and without becoming symptomatic.

Although you will perhaps be taking in more calories as you feel better, it can be challenging to try to put weight on without choosing unhealthy foods. Remember that on the low-FODMAP diet, you can safely eat protein-based foods such as fish, lean meats, and tofu. You can also choose to eat the following FODMAP-friendly foods that are good sources of healthy fats:

- Avocado (⅛ of whole per serving)
- Low-FODMAP nuts
- Low-FODMAP nut butters

An additional tip for gaining weight in a healthy way is to add an extra meal into your day. This way you do not have to stress your body with overly heavy meals just to try to increase your caloric intake. You can either choose to eat two lunches, spaced evenly through the time between breakfast and dinner, or have a more substantial late-evening snack.

The Low-FODMAP Diet for Vegetarians

If you are a vegetarian, you may have been dismayed to find that many of your go-to foods are restricted. This will be most evident in the restriction of legumes, but you may also be lamenting the loss of many of your other favorite vegetables. Keep in mind that your diet will be most restricted through the Elimination Phase. Once you are through that phase, you may find that you are better able to tolerate more of your normal foods. If you are not confident that you will be meeting all of your needs, please seek help from a qualified dietary professional.

Alternative Protein Sources

Taking in enough protein is essential for anyone following a vegetarian diet. However, with the restriction of legumes as part of the low-FODMAP diet, adequate protein consumption becomes even more challenging. If you are a lacto-ovo vegetarian, you can turn to eggs, hard cheeses, and lactose-free milk products. Additional protein-rich options for all types of vegetarians include:

- Low-FODMAP nuts and seeds
- Low-FODMAP milk substitutes
- Low-FODMAP grains
- Allowed soy products

Legumes

Don't forget that you do have the option of small servings of canned lentils (½ cup) and chickpeas (¼ cup) in all phases of the diet as long as they are drained and well rinsed. Once you have been through the Challenge Phase, you may find that you are better able to tolerate small amounts of other legumes.

As you move beyond the Elimination and Challenge Phases of the diet, keep in mind the notion of FODMAP load. Since legumes are such a good protein source, you may want to limit your intake of other high-FODMAP foods each day so as to allow your body to comfortably process your legume intake.

FACT

Although soybeans, soy flour, and soy milk must be restricted, tofu and tempeh are allowed due to the way they are prepared. You may want to check ingredients and assess your own sensitivity to tempeh. Seitan, also known as wheat gluten, is allowed on the diet because its preparation removes all FODMAPs. However, seitan is not an option if you have celiac disease.

The Low-FODMAP Diet for Children

As of this writing there is only preliminary research into whether the low-FODMAP diet can reduce abdominal pain in children with IBS. However, even though the research in this area is limited, there does not appear to be anything that would make it unadvisable to place a child on the diet.

Before starting, be sure to get clearance from your child's pediatrician or a pediatric gastroenterologist. You need to make sure that the digestive difficulties are properly diagnosed. Your child's doctor is also in the best position to judge whether the diet is appropriate given your child's overall health status.

For practical reasons, you may find that it is easier to utilize the One-by-One approach described in Chapter 4 rather than trying to get your child through a four- to eight-week Elimination Phase. As your child follows the diet, you need to be especially careful to ensure that vital nutritional needs are being fully addressed. For that reason, it's best to consult with a qualified dietitian.

Involve Your Child

One way to maximize the chances of a positive outcome of the diet is to get your child to play an active part in the whole process. Obviously the level of involvement will be determined by your child's age. The more the child is involved, the more likely he or she will be to adhere to the restrictions inherent in the diet. Using understandable terms, you can explain the science behind the diet. It will also be helpful to have your child participate in meal planning and snack buying. Engage the child in generating strategies for whatever situation may occur.

ESSENTIAL

When it comes to supervising your child on the low-FODMAP diet, don't sweat the small stuff. Occasionally eating small amounts of high-FODMAP foods will not put your child's health at risk the way a food allergy or celiac disease would. The child might experience some digestive symptoms, but this is a risk that he or she may choose to take (and hopefully learn from!).

Educate Other Adults

Be sure to discuss your child's dietary needs with the other adults who interact with him or her. This includes family members; school, camp, and athletic personnel; and the parents of your child's friends. Luckily, most people who work with children are now well aware of the need for dietary restrictions due to health conditions. When necessary, you can send your child out the door with FODMAP-appropriate foods for times spent away from home.

Healthy Living Tips

Your digestive and overall health require more than just following a diet in which you are limiting yourself to foods that are well tolerated. Your body is a system that functions as a whole; therefore, a holistic approach to your health will enhance the positive changes that the diet will bring. Try to make sure your life includes time for fun, spirituality, and relaxation. You may want to consider working with a health coach who is trained in supporting people in a holistic manner.

Choose Organic or Locally Grown Foods

Eating organic vegetables, fruits, and grains is not required as part of the low-FODMAP diet. However, if you are reading this book because you experience chronic digestive symptoms, you already know that you have a sensitive digestive system. Choosing to eat organically grown plant foods minimizes your intake of potentially harmful pesticides, fertilizers, and other chemicals.

Locally grown foods are also typically healthier than the conventionally grown vegetables and fruits that you find in supermarkets. Small farms often use significantly fewer chemicals to grow their foods, as they rely on old-school farming techniques of rotating and diversifying crops. Shop at farmers' markets and farm stands and chat with the farmers about their growing practices.

Limit Sugar

Although sugar in some of its various forms is allowed on the low-FODMAP diet, this doesn't mean that you should eat it freely. Overconsumption of sugar, both in sweet treats and as a hidden food ingredient, has contributed to the obesity epidemic in our society, as well as the rising rates of cardiovascular disease, diabetes, and cancer. Your overall health will benefit if you keep your sugar consumption to a minimum. This will give you the added benefit of keeping your fructose intake at a tolerable level.

One of the hidden perks of the low-FODMAP diet is that you will be greatly reducing your intake of refined carbohydrates in the form of processed wheat. To your body, refined carbohydrates are no different from simple sugar, and thus this ubiquitous ingredient is another reason for the rising rates of the chronic diseases already mentioned. You will be doing your body a great service as you swap out refined carbohydrates for the low-FODMAP whole grains that are allowed on the diet.

Physical Exercise

Have you found it hard to exercise due to your IBS? Following the low-FODMAP diet may open up new options for you as your body's functioning becomes more predictable and less disruptive. If you have never been much for exercise, use your new-found digestive health as a source of inspiration for overall self-care. Exercise is critical for your health, but it doesn't have to be a chore. There are so many ways to move your body—play around with various options until you find one that you enjoy.

Stress Management

Everyone's life has its own unique set of stressors. Hopefully, this low-FODMAP diet will knock IBS off of the top of your stress list! Stress management activities are things that you do to counterbalance the effect of the stresses in your life. Your stress can be eased just by the simple act of having a belly laugh or spending some time outdoors. More formal stress management activities include the following:

- Meditation
- Physical exercise
- Relaxation exercises
- Tai chi
- Yoga

The Recipes in This Book

The recipes in this book were designed with only low-FODMAP ingredients and thus are appropriate for all phases of the diet. Special care was taken to ensure that ingredients are readily available and don't have any hidden high-FODMAP elements. Each recipe includes wholesome, nutritious ingredients, with a special emphasis on whole foods whenever possible. You will see that the recipes provide you with options for eating an extremely wide variety of allowed foods to ensure that your fiber and other nutritional needs are met. In addition, you will see that many recipes were designed to be manageable in terms of time and effort so that you can cook healthy, delicious, low-FODMAP foods for yourself no matter how busy your life is.

Cooking should be an enjoyable, creative process. Feel free to add in or substitute any additional low-FODMAP ingredients that you enjoy and avoid using any ingredients that you know you have a personal sensitivity to. Once you have a better sense of which FODMAP types your body can handle, either through hydrogen breath testing (see Chapter 2) or through successful food challenges, you will have even more options to play with. Experiment and have fun!

ALERT

The designation of all ingredients as low-FODMAP was dependent upon the latest updates published by the researchers at Monash University, as well as other qualified sources, at the time this book was written. Recipes have not been individually evaluated for their overall FODMAP content.

For menu planning ideas and updates on allowed and restricted foods, please visit *www.EverythingLowFODMAP.com*.

CHAPTER 6

Breakfast

Baked French Toast

French toast is an indulgence that you need not give up because of a low-FODMAP diet. Prepared the night before, this is a recipe for a lazy weekend morning. Thirty minutes before serving, pop the whole dish in the oven, bake, and serve with maple syrup.

INGREDIENTS | SERVES 6

6 large eggs

2 cups lactose-free milk

2 tablespoons pure maple syrup

1 teaspoon pure vanilla extract

⅛ teaspoon sea salt

1 tablespoon ground cinnamon

6 slices gluten-free bread, lightly toasted

Milk Substitutes on the Low-FODMAP Diet

Many low-FODMAP recipes call for rice milk or lactose-free milk. The diet allows coconut, oat, rice, and lactose-free milks (check labels: only FODMAP-friendly additives allowed). You can choose based on taste preference, dietary needs, or whatever's in your refrigerator! Keep in mind, your choice—and its fat content—will influence the flavor and texture of your dish.

1. Coat a 13" × 9" baking dish with coconut oil spray. In a medium bowl, whisk together eggs, milk, syrup, vanilla, salt, and cinnamon.

2. Arrange bread to fill bottom of the baking dish—in 1 to 2 layers, trimming bread as necessary to fit. Pour liquid mixture evenly over the top. Cover and refrigerate overnight.

3. In the morning, preheat oven to 375°F. Bake for 30 minutes or until egg mixture is completely set. Let stand 5 minutes before serving.

PER SERVING | Calories: 230 | Fat: 8g | Protein: 12g | Sodium: 350mg | Fiber: 1g | Carbohydrates: 26g | Sugar: 8g

Peanut Butter Waffles

Teff is an ancient Ethiopian grain that is naturally gluten-free. Its flour adds a nice crunch to these protein-packed delights.

INGREDIENTS | SERVES 6

½ cup lactose-free milk

1 teaspoon white wine vinegar

¼ cup teff flour

¼ cup tapioca flour

1 cup gluten-free oat flour

1 teaspoon gluten-free baking powder

¼ teaspoon sea salt

1 large egg

½ cup natural peanut butter

2 tablespoons pure maple syrup

1 teaspoon unrefined coconut oil, liquefied

Maple Syrup, Pancake Syrup, and the Low-FODMAP Diet

Make sure you read the label on your pancake syrup. If it contains HFCS, it is not appropriate for the low-FODMAP diet. Purchase pure maple syrup to ensure that you are getting the real (and low-FODMAP!) version.

1. Mix milk with vinegar in a small bowl.

2. In a medium bowl, whisk together flours, baking powder, and salt.

3. In a mixer, blend egg, peanut butter, syrup, and oil. Stir in milk mixture.

4. Drizzle peanut butter mixture over flour mixture, stirring gently. Do not overmix.

5. Preheat waffle iron. Drop ¼ cup of batter into each section. Close lid and cook until waffle iron indicates ready. Repeat as necessary to use up batter. Serve immediately.

PER SERVING | Calories: 275 | Fat: 14g | Protein: 10g | Sodium: 300mg | Fiber: 3g | Carbohydrates: 29g | Sugar: 7g

Pumpkin Pancakes

Hot off the griddle, these pancakes are surprisingly light and fluffy for being gluten-free.
If your canned pumpkin is very gelatinous, whisk in a few tablespoons of water.

INGREDIENTS | SERVES 6

1 tablespoon rice milk

1 teaspoon white wine vinegar

2 tablespoons coconut flour

1 cup gluten-free oat flour

1 teaspoon gluten-free baking powder

⅛ teaspoon sea salt

1 teaspoon ground cinnamon

¼ cup canned pumpkin

2 large eggs

2 tablespoons pure maple syrup

1 tablespoon plus 1 teaspoon unrefined coconut oil, liquefied and divided

1 teaspoon pure vanilla extract

1. Mix milk with vinegar in a small bowl.

2. In a large bowl, whisk together flours, baking powder, salt, and cinnamon.

3. In a medium bowl, whisk pumpkin, eggs, syrup, 1 tablespoon oil, and vanilla. Stir in milk mixture.

4. Drizzle pumpkin mixture over flour mixture, stirring gently. Do not overmix.

5. Heat a large skillet or griddle over medium heat. Grease skillet with remaining oil. Divide batter into six evenly scooped pancakes.

6. Cook for 2 minutes. Flip once undersides are fully cooked. Cook 2 minutes more until pancakes are fully cooked. Serve immediately.

PER SERVING | Calories: 135 | Fat: 6g | Protein: 5g | Sodium: 150mg | Fiber: 3g | Carbohydrates: 17g | Sugar: 4g

Brownie Pancakes

Brownie Pancakes are rich and dense enough to be called dessert—but so good for you! Enjoy with a drizzle of dark amber maple syrup or a dollop of natural peanut butter.

INGREDIENTS | SERVES 6

½ cup lactose-free milk

1 tablespoon white wine vinegar

1 cup gluten-free oat flour

¼ cup buckwheat flour

½ cup raw cacao powder

1 teaspoon gluten-free baking powder

½ teaspoon allspice

¼ teaspoon sea salt

½ ripe banana, peeled, mashed

1 teaspoon pure vanilla extract

1 tablespoon blackstrap molasses

2 tablespoons pure maple syrup

1 large egg

1 tablespoon plus 1 teaspoon unrefined coconut oil, liquefied and divided

Gluten-Free Baking Tip

Gluten is an important ingredient for baking because it helps dough to rise. One of the challenges of gluten-free baking is ensuring that the dough will rise sufficiently; otherwise, the result can be too dense. One trick is to mix vinegar into some lactose-free milk. Folded gently into batter, this mixture helps add air and rise to baked goods.

1. Mix milk with vinegar in a small bowl.

2. In a medium bowl, whisk together flours, cacao powder, baking powder, allspice, and salt.

3. In a mixer, combine banana, vanilla, molasses, maple syrup, egg, and 1 tablespoon of oil. Stir in milk mixture by hand.

4. Drizzle banana mixture over flour mixture, stirring gently. Do not overmix.

5. Heat a large skillet or griddle over medium heat. Grease skillet with remaining oil.

6. For each pancake, scoop ⅙ of the batter onto skillet. Gently adjust shape as necessary into circular pancake form—but do not flatten.

7. Cook each pancake for 2 minutes. Flip once undersides are fully cooked. Cook 2 minutes more until pancakes are fully cooked. Serve immediately.

PER SERVING | Calories: 175 | Fat: 7g | Protein: 6g | Sodium: 200mg | Fiber: 4g | Carbohydrates: 27g | Sugar: 9g

Amaranth Breakfast

This recipe will make your home smell wonderful! This is a nice recipe to cook in a rice cooker, if you happen to have one. When serving, feel free to add a few drops of maple syrup and whatever berries you have on hand.

INGREDIENTS | SERVES 4

1 cup amaranth seeds

3 cups water

2 teaspoons ground cinnamon

1 tablespoon pure vanilla extract

¼ cup shelled pecans, lightly chopped

1. Heat a heavy-bottomed saucepan over medium heat and add amaranth. Toast amaranth, stirring occasionally for 5 minutes until fragrant.

2. Pour in 3 cups water and bring to a boil. Lower heat and add cinnamon and vanilla. Cover, then simmer for 20 minutes, stirring occasionally.

3. While amaranth is simmering, place pecans under broiler for 4 minutes to toast.

4. When amaranth has finished cooking, give it a good stir and remove from heat. Serve in bowls topped with the pecans.

PER SERVING | Calories: 230 | Fat: 5g | Protein: 6g | Sodium: 5mg | Fiber: 9g | Carbohydrates: 41g | Sugar: 1g

Cream of Muesli

Once you have made the basic recipe, you have options for making your muesli even more nutritious and delicious. Enjoy some healthy decadence with a swirl of natural peanut butter, topped with sliced banana and a sprinkle of cacao powder.

INGREDIENTS | MAKES 6½ CUPS

½ cup hulled pumpkin seeds
½ cup hulled sunflower seeds
½ cup shelled walnuts
3 cups rolled gluten-free oats
1 cup gluten-free oat bran
¼ cup buckwheat flour
½ cup finely ground flaxseeds
½ cup finely ground chia seeds
1 tablespoon ground cinnamon
6½ cups lactose-free milk

1. Add all ingredients except milk to a food processor.

2. Pulse 20 or 30 times. Scrape sides of the work bowl. Pulse 20 to 30 times more, until all seeds and nuts appear chopped to a coarse consistency.

3. For each serving, scoop ½ cup of muesli into a small saucepan and add ½ cup of milk. Bring to a simmer over medium heat and stir for 2–3 minutes.

4. Transfer to a breakfast bowl and serve.

PER SERVING (½ CUP) | Calories: 325 | Fat: 18g | Protein: 14g | Sodium: 55mg | Fiber: 9g | Carbohydrates: 32g | Sugar: 7g

Grinding Seeds

As you follow the low-FODMAP diet, you may find yourself experimenting with some new seeds. Both flaxseeds and chia seeds are good sources of dietary fiber and anti-inflammatory omega-3 fatty acids. Flaxseeds need to be ground before eating. Invest in a little coffee grinder and dedicate it to the easy task of seed grinding.

Dressed-Up Eggs

This quick and easy recipe is not only a great way to start your day, but also makes an impressive main course for company brunch. Be sure to rinse the sprouts thoroughly for a solid 2 minutes, and then drain and dry before using.

INGREDIENTS | SERVES 4

8 large eggs

1 teaspoon unrefined coconut oil, liquefied

1 medium tomato, seeded and diced

¼ teaspoon sea salt

¼ teaspoon freshly ground black pepper

¾ cup alfalfa sprouts

1 tablespoon chopped fresh flat-leaf parsley

1 tablespoon hulled pumpkin seeds

1 tablespoon hulled sunflower seeds

Coconut Oil Tip

When baking with coconut oil—whether it be a breakfast or dessert recipe—it is important to make sure that you bring other ingredients to room temperature, e.g., milk, egg, and yogurt. This helps to prevent the liquefied coconut oil from clumping in the mixing process.

1. In a medium bowl, whisk eggs.

2. Heat oil in a medium skillet over medium heat. Swirl oil to coat skillet. Add eggs to skillet and cook for 1 minute. Stir gently until eggs are completely cooked, about 1 minute more. Move scrambled eggs to a plate and cover to keep warm.

3. Add diced tomato to skillet and sauté over medium heat 3–5 minutes. Season with salt and pepper.

4. Divide eggs evenly onto four breakfast plates. Top eggs with tomatoes and sprouts, sprinkle with parsley and seeds, and serve.

PER SERVING | Calories: 185 | Fat: 13g | Protein: 14g | Sodium: 290mg | Fiber: 1g | Carbohydrates: 3g | Sugar: 2g

Lemon Pepper Omelet

Surprise your morning taste buds with the unique flavors in this quick, easy, and protein-packed egg dish.

INGREDIENTS | SERVES 1

1 teaspoon fresh lemon juice

1 teaspoon fresh lemon zest

2 teaspoons extra-virgin olive oil, divided

⅛ teaspoon sea salt

⅛ teaspoon freshly ground black pepper

1 cup fresh arugula

2 medium eggs

¼ teaspoon ground turmeric

1 teaspoon freshly grated Parmesan cheese

1. In a small bowl or jar, make dressing: Whisk together lemon juice, zest, 1 teaspoon of oil, salt, and pepper.

2. Heat dressing in a medium skillet over medium heat. Add arugula and sauté, until just starting to wilt (do not overcook). Remove skillet from heat.

3. In a small bowl, whisk eggs and turmeric.

4. In a small skillet, swirl remaining teaspoon of oil over medium heat until hot. Add egg mixture and cook for 30 seconds. Top with arugula mixture and sprinkle with Parmesan.

5. Cook for 2 minutes or until underside is fully set. Flip omelet over and cook 1 minute more, or to desired doneness. Serve immediately.

PER SERVING | Calories: 220 | Fat: 18g | Protein: 13g | Sodium: 465mg | Fiber: 1g | Carbohydrates: 2g | Sugar: 1g

Lazy Susan Oatmeal

Make a simple oatmeal breakfast more fun by setting up a lazy Susan with a variety of delicious, nutritious toppings. Other combination ideas include fresh cranberries, pecans, and pumpkin seeds; or fresh strawberry slices, macadamia nuts, and dark chocolate chips.

INGREDIENTS | SERVES 4

3½ cups lactose-free milk

2 cups gluten-free rolled oats

1 teaspoon pure vanilla extract

1 teaspoon ground cinnamon

½ cup blueberries

½ cup shelled, chopped walnuts

½ cup lactose-free yogurt

½ cup freshly ground flaxseeds

½ cup shredded unsweetened coconut

1. In a medium saucepan, heat milk over low heat.

2. Add oats and vanilla and cook for 5 minutes, stirring occasionally. Divide oatmeal evenly into 4 breakfast bowls. Sprinkle cinnamon evenly over each bowl of oatmeal.

3. Put remaining ingredients into their own small bowls. Transfer small bowls, with complementary serving spoons, to a 10" lazy Susan serving tray.

4. Set tray in center of table. Set a bowl of oatmeal in front of each diner and encourage everyone to choose their own toppings.

PER SERVING | Calories: 515 | Fat: 28g | Protein: 19g | Sodium: 110mg | Fiber: 11g | Carbohydrates: 50g | Sugar: 16g

Crunchy Granola

This smells so good when it is cooking in the oven! Make a big batch of this mega-healthy granola on the weekend and then enjoy it all week as a quick and easy breakfast or snack.

INGREDIENTS | SERVES 12

4 cups gluten-free rolled oats

½ cup sliced almonds

1 cup hulled sunflower seeds

½ cup pure maple syrup

3 tablespoons unrefined coconut oil, liquefied

2 teaspoons pure vanilla extract

2 teaspoons ground cinnamon

½ teaspoon sea salt

1. Preheat oven to 325°F.

2. Mix all ingredients in a large bowl. Transfer mixture to a baking sheet lined with parchment paper.

3. Cook for 50 minutes, stirring every 10–15 minutes.

PER SERVING | Calories: 260 | Fat: 13g | Protein: 7g | Sodium: 100mg | Fiber: 4g | Carbohydrates: 31g | Sugar: 9g

Liquefying Coconut Oil

Coconut oil will change from solid to liquid depending on the room temperature. To liquefy, heat up a burner. Place desired amount of oil in a small pot. Turn off burner and place pot on heated burner. (If you do not like the taste of or are allergic to coconut, you can substitute olive oil or melted butter.)

Quinoa "Carrot Cake" Breakfast

Feel free to treat yourself to dessert for breakfast, with this healthy spin on a bakery classic. If you like sweets, feel free to drizzle some maple syrup on your bowl.

INGREDIENTS | SERVES 6

1 cup uncooked quinoa, rinsed

1½ cups filtered water

2 carrots, peeled, grated

¼ cup shelled walnuts, chopped

1 tablespoon ground cinnamon

¼ teaspoon sea salt

Whole Grains and the Low-FODMAP Diet

As wheat is not allowed on the diet, you will want to acquaint yourself with some new whole grain and seed options, such as amaranth, buckwheat, millet, quinoa, sorghum, and teff. Spelt is considered low-FODMAP but is not gluten-free. All flours made from approved ingredients, e.g. gluten-free oats and corn (polenta) are allowed on the diet.

1. Place quinoa in a medium saucepan along with 1½ cups of filtered water and bring to a boil over high heat. Reduce heat to low, cover, and simmer for 10 minutes.

2. Add carrots, walnuts, cinnamon, and salt to quinoa and continue simmering, covered, for another 10 minutes.

PER SERVING | Calories: 145 | Fat: 5g | Protein: 5g | Sodium: 115mg | Fiber: 3g | Carbohydrates: 22g | Sugar: 1g

Savory Sourdough Strata

Prepared the night before, a strata is an easy weekend brunch main dish.

INGREDIENTS | SERVES 8

1 tablespoon extra-virgin olive oil

10 ounces packed baby spinach leaves

1 teaspoon sea salt, divided

2 cups Roasted Tomato Sauce (see recipe in Chapter 9)

5 cups gluten-free sourdough bread, crusts removed, insides cut to 1" cubes

6 large eggs

1½ cups lactose-free milk

1 cup shredded sharp Cheddar cheese, divided

¼ teaspoon freshly ground black pepper

4 slices cooked, cooled, chopped bacon

What about Sourdough?

Traditional sourdough is produced through a process of fermentation, which reduces its FODMAP fructans level. However, many commercial sourdough products use baker's yeast to get a rise to save the time needed for the fermentation process. To ensure that the sourdough bread you are eating is low in FODMAP, choose either a gluten-free option or a traditionally prepared artisanal sourdough.

1. Heat oil in a medium skillet over medium heat.

2. Add spinach and pinch of salt, and sauté until wilted. Set aside to cool.

3. Mix cooled spinach with Roasted Tomato Sauce and spread in a thin layer at the bottom of a 13" × 9" baking dish. Top with bread cubes.

4. Separately, in a medium bowl, whisk eggs, milk, ½ cup cheese, remaining salt, and pepper. Pour evenly over bread cubes. Hand-turn to coat any dry cubes—ensuring they are all wet. Sprinkle evenly with remaining cheese and bacon. Cover and refrigerate overnight.

5. In the morning, heat oven to 375°F. Bake uncovered for 30–40 minutes, or until cheese melts and egg mixture is fully set.

PER SERVING | Calories: 475 | Fat: 22g | Protein: 22g | Sodium: 1,600mg | Fiber: 4g | Carbohydrates: 50g | Sugar: 10g

Cuppa Coffee Cake

The low-FODMAP diet allows one cup of coffee per day. Linger over yours with this sweet breakfast treat. Rounding out your plate with a handful of walnuts and lactose-free plain yogurt will help ward off the temptation to take seconds!

INGREDIENTS | SERVES 9

1 cup turbinado sugar, divided

2¼ cups gluten-free oat flour, divided

1 teaspoon ground cinnamon

2 tablespoons butter, softened, divided

¼ cup coconut flour

1 teaspoon gluten-free baking powder

½ teaspoon baking soda

⅛ teaspoon sea salt

2 tablespoons unrefined coconut oil, softened

1 large egg

¾ cup lactose-free milk

¼ cup lactose-free plain yogurt

1 teaspoon white wine vinegar

What Is Turbinado Sugar?

In moderation, sugar is allowed on the low-FODMAP diet. Turbinado sugar is a slightly healthier sugar than the more commonly used refined white sugar. It's minimally processed, so its crystals are larger and slightly golden in hue. You can use turbinado sugar in place of white sugar in equal amounts.

1. Preheat oven to 350°F. Line an 8" × 8" baking dish with parchment paper and spray with coconut oil spray.

2. Process ¼ cup turbinado sugar in a coffee grinder until powdered.

3. Make the topping: In a bowl, combine powdered turbinado sugar, ¼ cup oat flour, and cinnamon. Using your hands, work in 1 tablespoon of butter until medium clumps form alongside smaller ones.

4. In a large bowl, combine remaining oat flour, coconut flour, baking powder, baking soda, and salt.

5. In a mixer, cream remaining ¾ cup sugar with 1 tablespoon butter and coconut oil. Add egg, milk, and yogurt. By hand, stir vinegar into milk mixture.

6. Drizzle wet ingredients over flour mixture, stirring gently. Do not overmix.

7. Pour batter into baking dish. Sprinkle topping evenly over batter.

8. Bake 20 minutes or until topping begins to brown and a toothpick inserted and removed from cake's center remains clean.

PER SERVING | Calories: 290 | Fat: 10g | Protein: 7g | Sodium: 180mg | Fiber: 4g | Carbohydrates: 47g | Sugar: 24g

Cranberry Orange Scones

If you enjoy a challenge, these are super-fun to bake. To simplify—with an equally delectable result—divide the batter evenly in a lined muffin pan and then bake as directed. Although fruit juices are not typically allowed on the diet, the amount of orange juice in this recipe is small enough so as not to cause a problem.

INGREDIENTS | SERVES 12

3 cups gluten-free oat flour, divided

1 tablespoon rice milk

1 teaspoon white wine vinegar

2 tablespoons plus 1 teaspoon dried orange zest, divided

¾ cup plus 1 teaspoon turbinado sugar, divided

¼ teaspoon ground cinnamon

¼ cup coconut flour

¼ cup freshly ground flaxseeds

1 teaspoon gluten-free baking powder

½ teaspoon baking soda

⅛ teaspoon sea salt

½ cup orange juice

2 tablespoons unrefined coconut oil, liquefied

1 teaspoon pure vanilla extract

¼ cup dried cranberries, chopped

1 large egg

Make Your Own Nutritive Flours

Many of the nutritive, gluten-free flours included in recipe ingredient lists can be easily made at home for a cost savings. For example, to make oat flour, run gluten-free rolled oats through a food processor to a flour consistency. If you prefer baking with white flour, you may substitute all-purpose gluten-free flour in any recipe.

1. Preheat oven to 350°F. Line 2 baking sheets with parchment. Cover a work surface with a large square of parchment dusted with ½ cup oat flour.

2. Mix milk with vinegar in a small bowl.

3. In a small bowl, mix 1 teaspoon each zest and sugar. Add cinnamon.

4. In a large bowl, mix 2 cups oat flour, coconut flour, flaxseeds, remaining zest, baking powder, baking soda, and salt.

5. In a mixer, blend juice, oil, vanilla, and cranberries. Add egg and blend again. By hand, stir in milk mixture.

6. Drizzle wet ingredients over flour mixture, stirring gently. Do not overmix. Allow dough to rise and thicken, about 5 minutes.

7. Gently scoop ½ cup of batter onto floured workspace. With floured hands, turn dough very gently over to coat all sides. Do not knead dough. Carefully transfer flour-coated dough to a lined baking sheet and gently shape into a triangle. (Dough will spread; give it lots of height.) Repeat—adding oat flour as needed to workspace—until all dough is transferred to baking sheets and shaped into triangles.

8. Sprinkle the top of each scone with a pinch of cinnamon mixture.

9. Bake 18–20 minutes, or until tops are starting to brown. Serve warm.

PER SERVING | Calories: 230 | Fat: 7g | Protein: 6g | Sodium: 130mg | Fiber: 5g | Carbohydrates: 39g | Sugar: 15g

Coconut Zucchini Muffins

This recipe takes a classic treat and packs it with some super-nutrition! Enjoy for breakfast or a late-day tea break. This also makes a great take-along item for parties or playdates.

INGREDIENTS | SERVES 12

1 medium zucchini, hand grated
1 tablespoon lactose-free milk
1 teaspoon white wine vinegar
2 cups all-purpose, gluten-free flour
2 tablespoons coconut flour
1/4 cup shaved coconut
1 teaspoon gluten-free baking powder
1/2 teaspoon baking soda
1 teaspoon ground cinnamon
1/8 teaspoon sea salt
3/4 cup demerara sugar
1 teaspoon blackstrap molasses
1 teaspoon pure vanilla extract
1/4 cup lactose-free plain yogurt
1/4 cup unrefined coconut oil, liquefied
1 large egg

What Is Demerara Sugar?

Demerara sugar is a slightly healthier sugar than the more commonly used refined brown sugar. It's minimally processed with some molasses left in—so its color is deeper in hue and its flavor lends a hint of toffee. You can use demerara sugar in place of light brown sugar in equal amounts.

1. Heat oven to 375°F. Prepare a muffin pan with coconut oil spray or liners.

2. Using a colander, squeeze as much liquid as possible out of grated zucchini.

3. In a small bowl, whisk together milk and vinegar.

4. In a large bowl, whisk together flours, coconut, baking powder, baking soda, cinnamon, and salt.

5. In a mixer, blend sugar, molasses, vanilla, yogurt, oil, egg, and zucchini. By hand, stir in milk mixture.

6. Drizzle zucchini mixture over flour mixture, stirring gently just until combined. Do not overmix. Divide batter evenly in muffin pan.

7. Bake 18–20 minutes or until a toothpick inserted and removed from center remains clean.

PER SERVING | Calories: 185 | Fat: 6g | Protein: 3g | Sodium: 125mg | Fiber: 2g | Carbohydrates: 31g | Sugar: 14g

Lunch

Turkey Cranberry Panini

If you have a panini maker, by all means use it to press and cook this hot sandwich for lunch. Otherwise, follow the recipe for similar results.

INGREDIENTS | SERVES 1

1 tablespoon dried cranberries
1 teaspoon walnut oil
2 slices gluten-free bread, lightly toasted
1 (1") cube Cheddar cheese, sliced thin
2 slices deli turkey
1 teaspoon country Dijon mustard
¼ teaspoon dried thyme

1. Soak the cranberries in boiling water for 10 minutes to soften, then drain.

2. Melt half the oil in the center of a medium skillet over medium-low heat. Top with 1 slice of toast, then cheese, cranberries, and turkey. Spread mustard on second slice of toast, sprinkle with thyme, and place atop the turkey.

3. Using a flat, handled pot lid, press down on sandwich as it cooks. When underside is evenly browned, lift sandwich, add remaining oil to skillet, flip sandwich over, and press again. Cook until cheese starts to melt and underside is evenly browned.

4. Remove from skillet and serve immediately.

PER SERVING | Calories: 444 | Fat: 18g | Protein: 27g | Sodium: 675mg | Fiber: 2g | Carbohydrates: 43g | Sugar: 7g

Peanut Butter and "Jam" Sandwich

Sadly, jellies and jams are not low in FODMAPs. But by creating this quick "jam," you can still enjoy a classic childhood comfort food. You can make a larger batch of "jam" ahead of time, so that your actual meal prep time will be minimal.

INGREDIENTS | SERVES 1

½ cup hulled strawberries, quartered

1 tablespoon natural peanut butter

2 slices gluten-free bread

1. Cook berries in a small saucepan for 5 minutes or until soft and syrupy. Let cool.

2. Top bread or toast with peanut butter and "jam" and serve.

PER SERVING | Calories: 300 | Fat: 9g | Protein: 12g | Sodium: 490mg | Fiber: 4g | Carbohydrates: 45g | Sugar: 7g

Cucumber and Egg Sandwiches

You can cut the crusts off the bread and serve this for tea, or leave them on for a satisfying lunch. Gluten-free bread can be crumbly, so be sure to allow time for the butter to soften. Add a handful of spinach leaves to each sandwich for an extra nutritional punch.

INGREDIENTS | SERVES 4

2 large hard-cooked eggs, shelled

1 tablespoon full-fat mayonnaise

¼ teaspoon paprika

1 tablespoon butter, softened

8 slices gluten-free bread

⅓ English cucumber (approximately 4 inches), thinly sliced

1 tablespoon chopped fresh dill

1. In a small bowl, mash eggs, mayonnaise, and paprika with a fork to desired consistency.

2. Lightly butter all 8 slices of bread.

3. Assemble sandwiches: Arrange cucumber slices on the butter side of 4 slices of bread. Top with egg mixture and sprinkle with dill. Cover with another slice of bread, butter side down.

PER SERVING | Calories: 270 | Fat: 9g | Protein: 11g | Sodium: 470mg | Fiber: 2g | Carbohydrates: 37g | Sugar: 2g

Niçoise Wraps

*For a quick, healthy lunch to go, wrap fillings can be prepared ahead
and wrapped in lettuce leaves just prior to serving.*

INGREDIENTS | SERVES 4

1 tablespoon extra-virgin olive oil

1 teaspoon white wine vinegar

½ teaspoon Dijon mustard

⅛ teaspoon sea salt

⅛ teaspoon freshly ground black pepper

4 large butter lettuce leaves

1 (5-ounce) can tuna, drained, flaked

1 large hard-cooked egg, shelled and diced

1 cup green beans, trimmed to 1" pieces, blanched

1 large tomato, seeded and diced

8 Kalamata olives, pitted and diced

1. In a small dish, make the dressing: Whisk oil, vinegar, mustard, salt, and pepper.

2. Lay lettuce leaves on a flat serving dish. Fill each leaf with 2 tablespoons tuna, 1 tablespoon egg, ¼ cup green beans, 1 tablespoon tomato, and 1 teaspoon olives. Drizzle each with dressing.

3. Wrap lettuce securely around filling and serve.

PER SERVING | Calories: 168 | Fat: 8g | Protein: 13g | Sodium: 230mg | Fiber: 2g | Carbohydrates: 12g | Sugar: 2g

Tuna Melt "Nachos"

Who says lunch can't be fun? Break up your day with a little fiesta—you'll get in some of your veggies for the day while enjoying the feeling of confidence that your system can handle these FODMAP-friendly ingredients.

INGREDIENTS | SERVES 1

1 small (3-ounce) can tuna, drained, flaked

1 medium carrot, peeled and sliced into ½" rounds

1 teaspoon full-fat mayonnaise

1 teaspoon lactose-free yogurt

⅛ teaspoon sea salt

⅛ teaspoon freshly ground black pepper

8 gluten-free nacho chips

1 cup loosely packed baby spinach leaves

¼ cup grated Swiss cheese

1. Preheat broiler. In a food processor, mix tuna, carrot, mayonnaise, yogurt, salt, and pepper.

2. On a broiler-safe tray, arrange nacho chips and top with a thin layer of baby spinach. Crumble tuna salad over spinach and top with Swiss cheese.

3. Broil 1–2 minutes, until cheese is melted. Cool slightly and serve.

PER SERVING | Calories: 440 | Fat: 23g | Protein: 31g | Sodium: 650mg | Fiber: 4g | Carbohydrates: 27g | Sugar: 5g

Full-Fat Mayonnaise and the Low-FODMAP Diet

It is a good idea to purchase full-fat mayonnaise while following the diet. Light mayonnaise can contain high fructose corn syrup (HFCS), which is not allowed on the diet due to its obviously high fructose level. Always read ingredient labels carefully. If you are worried about fat, just keep your portion size small.

Spinach Salad with Hot Bacon Dressing

Honey is the usual star of this sweet 'n' savory salad dish—but subbing in pure maple syrup makes it FODMAP-friendly (and finger-licking good). The bacon acts as a flavor agent: A little goes a long way.

INGREDIENTS | SERVES 4

¾ cup pure maple syrup

¼ cup arrowroot powder

¼ cup white wine vinegar

¼ cup orange juice

1 teaspoon orange zest

⅛ teaspoon sea salt

2 slices cooked, cooled, crumbled bacon

2 cups packed baby spinach leaves

2 hard-cooked eggs, shelled and chopped

1 cup shredded carrot

1. In a small saucepan over medium-low heat, whisk syrup, arrowroot, vinegar, juice, zest, and salt. Bring just to a boil, then simmer uncovered 5 minutes or until dressing has thickened. Remove from heat and stir in bacon.

2. While dressing is simmering, divide spinach into 4 serving bowls. Top each with chopped eggs and shredded carrots.

3. Drizzle 2 tablespoons of hot dressing over each salad bowl and serve immediately.

PER SERVING | Calories: 298 | Fat: 8g | Protein: 5g | Sodium: 240mg | Fiber: 1g | Carbohydrates: 52g | Sugar: 39g

What Is Arrowroot Powder?

Arrowroot powder is a powdery starch that comes from the roots of the arrowroot plant. Although to date it has not been tested for FODMAP content, it is easily digested and gluten-free and so is allowed during all phases of the diet. Arrowroot is a great thickening agent.

Savory Salad Granola

Granola is not just for breakfast anymore. Just a sprinkle of this more savory than sweet version adds a nutritious, flavorful crunch to lunch or dinner salads.

INGREDIENTS | MAKES 4 CUPS

1½ cups gluten-free rolled oats

½ cup shredded unsweetened coconut

½ cup shelled, chopped walnuts

⅛ teaspoon sea salt

⅛ cup blackstrap molasses

⅛ cup orange juice

¼ cup unrefined coconut oil, liquefied

¼ cup dried orange zest

¼ cup ground flaxseeds

1. Preheat oven to 350°F. Line a baking sheet with parchment paper.

2. In a large bowl, mix oats, coconut, walnuts, and salt.

3. In a separate, smaller bowl, whisk molasses and juice. Add oil, zest, and flaxseeds and stir until combined.

4. Stir molasses mixture into oats mixture and stir until combined.

5. Spread granola onto baking sheet in one thin layer. Bake 10 minutes. Remove tray from oven, stir granola, and return to oven for 10 minutes more.

6. Remove from oven and allow to cool completely.

PER SERVING (2 TABLESPOONS) | Calories: 105 | Fat: 8g | Protein: 2g | Sodium: 20mg | Fiber: 2g | Carbohydrates: 8g | Sugar: 2g

Carrot and Ginger Soup (Chapter 8)

Cranberry Walnut Balls (Chapter 15)

Peanut Butter Waffles (Chapter 6)

Chinese Chicken (Chapter 11)

Maple Molasses Trail Mix (Chapter 15)

Gingerbread Cupcakes with
Candied Ginger Frosting (Chapter 14)

Turkey Cranberry Panini (Chapter 7)

Peppermint Patties (Chapter 14)

Macaroni and Cheese (Chapter 10)

Colorful Penne Toss (Chapter 10)

Golden Changria (Chapter 16)

Toasted Coconut Almond Millet
(Chapter 13)

Rosemary Chicken Salad (Chapter 7)

Ice Cream Sandwiches (Chapter 14)

Pumpkin Pancakes (Chapter 6)

Pumpkin Cinnamon Cups (Chapter 16)

Arugula Salad with Melon (Chapter 13)

Garden Pesto (Chapter 9)

Almost Classic Hummus (Chapter 15)

Coconut Shrimp (Chapter 12)
with Kiwi Dipping Sauce (Chapter 9)

Scampi Primavera Sauce (Chapter 9)

Feta Crab Cakes (Chapter 12) with Tzatziki Dressing (Chapter 9)

Bolognese Sauce (Chapter 9)

Crunchy Granola (Chapter 6)

Spinach and Orange Salad

Feel free to top this colorful salad with Savory Salad Granola (see recipe in this chapter) for a filling lunch, bursting with tantalizing taste and texture.

INGREDIENTS | SERVES 1

1 cup packed baby spinach leaves
½ medium orange, peeled and diced
1 teaspoon extra-virgin olive oil
1 teaspoon red wine vinegar
1 teaspoon orange juice
½ teaspoon Dijon mustard
½ teaspoon sea salt

1. Toss spinach and orange pieces in a salad bowl.

2. In a separate small bowl make the dressing by whisking together the oil, vinegar, orange juice, mustard, and salt.

3. Pour over salad, toss to combine, and serve.

PER SERVING | Calories: 82 | Fat: 5g | Protein: 2g | Sodium: 1,200mg | Fiber: 2g | Carbohydrates: 10g | Sugar: 7g

Fruit Juice and the Low-FODMAP Diet

When following the low-FODMAP diet, it is safest to try to avoid fruit juice altogether, as the FODMAP load tends to be higher in juices than in the actual fruit. However, very small amounts of juice from low-FODMAP foods are allowed. Cranberry juice and tomato-based vegetable juices have been found to be low-FODMAP.

Lentil Salad over Arugula

This salad is a delightful, filling, and super-nutritious lunch. The sweetness of the dressing mellows out the bitterness of the arugula.

INGREDIENTS | SERVES 4

4 tablespoons roughly chopped shelled pecans

8 cups arugula

2 (15-ounce) cans lentils, drained and rinsed

1 medium red bell pepper, seeded and diced

2 tablespoons dried cranberries

½ cup Maple Mustard Salad Dressing (see recipe in this chapter)

1. Preheat broiler. Place pecans on rimmed baking sheet and toast for 3 minutes.

2. Divide arugula onto 4 salad plates. Equally divide up the lentils, bell pepper, pecans, and cranberries and place on top of the arugula. Drizzle dressing over salad and toss before serving.

PER SERVING | Calories: 675 | Fat: 33g | Protein: 27g | Sodium: 135mg | Fiber: 32g | Carbohydrates: 70g | Sugar: 9g

Raw Vegetables and the Low-FODMAP Diet

The low-FODMAP diet does not make any distinction between raw and cooked vegetables, as it is the carbohydrates within the vegetables that are theorized to contribute to IBS symptoms. However, many people with IBS have found that raw vegetables can be problematic. Processing vegetables before eating may make them more tolerable.

Maple Mustard Salad Dressing

You can whip up this dressing in moments, adding an elegant touch to any salad. Dressing can be stored in the refrigerator for up to one week. Let it come to room temperature before serving.

INGREDIENTS | MAKES 1 CUP

½ cup extra-virgin olive oil

2 tablespoons brown mustard

2 tablespoons pure maple syrup

2 tablespoons red wine vinegar

1 lemon, juiced

⅛ teaspoon sea salt

⅛ teaspoon freshly ground black pepper

Blend all ingredients until smooth.

PER SERVING (2 TABLESPOONS) | Calories: 135 | Fat: 14g | Protein: 0g | Sodium: 80mg | Fiber: 0g | Carbohydrates: 4g | Sugar: 3g

Quinoa with Canadian Bacon and Kale

This quinoa dish is perfect for lunch, but it also makes a great side dish. Pair it with some broiled chicken or steak and you have all of your bases covered for a complete dinner. Leave out the bacon and you have a delicious vegetarian option.

INGREDIENTS | SERVES 6

2 tablespoons extra-virgin olive oil, divided

2 cups uncooked quinoa, rinsed

4¼ cups water, divided

1 (6-ounce) package Canadian bacon, diced

1 medium red bell pepper, seeded and diced

1 bunch kale, stemmed and coarsely chopped

1 pinch crushed red pepper

⅛ teaspoon sea salt

⅛ teaspoon freshly ground black pepper

¼ cup freshly grated Parmesan cheese

Why Should Quinoa Be Rinsed Before Cooking?

A substance called saponin forms a coating on quinoa, which can make the seeds taste bitter or soapy. Rinsing the seeds before cooking dissolves the saponin. Be sure to use a fine-mesh strainer, as quinoa seeds are small.

1. Heat 1 tablespoon of the olive oil in a saucepan over medium-high heat. Add quinoa and stir for 5 minutes until it starts to toast, pop, and smell nice and nutty.

2. Pour 4 cups of filtered water into the quinoa pot and bring to a boil. Turn heat to low, cover, and simmer for 15 minutes until all water is absorbed. Let stand for 5 minutes.

3. While quinoa is simmering, heat remaining oil in a large skillet over medium-high heat. Add the Canadian bacon and sauté for 2 minutes, stirring. Add the red bell pepper and continue to sauté for an additional 8 minutes. Add the kale and crushed red pepper and sauté until kale is wilted, approximately 1 minute. Pour in ¼ cup of filtered water, cover, and steam for approximately 8 minutes until kale is softened.

4. Fluff quinoa with a fork and stir into the kale mixture. Season with salt and pepper. Stir in Parmesan cheese.

PER SERVING | Calories: 340 | Fat: 11g | Protein: 17g | Sodium: 540mg | Fiber: 5g | Carbohydrates: 43g | Sugar: 1g

Vegetable Frittata

This is an extremely versatile recipe; it can be an elegant everyday lunch or a hearty breakfast or light dinner. You can cook the frittatas one at a time if you don't have two broiler-proof skillets handy.

INGREDIENTS | SERVES 4

2 tablespoons extra-virgin olive oil, divided

1 (6-ounce) package of Canadian bacon, diced, divided

1 zucchini, diced, divided

1 red bell pepper, seeded and diced, divided

2 teaspoons dried basil, divided

2 teaspoons dried oregano, divided

1/8 teaspoon freshly ground black pepper, divided

1/8 teaspoon sea salt, divided

6 medium eggs

2 tablespoons water, divided

1/4 cup freshly grated Parmesan cheese, divided

Go Organic with Your Eggs

There are compelling reasons to buy organic eggs even for people who have hardy digestive systems. Organic eggs are higher in those super-healthy omega-3 fatty acids, and are free from the antibiotics and hormones found in nonorganic eggs. You are choosing to follow a low-FODMAP diet because you want to feel better—no need to take in unnecessary, and potentially harmful, extraneous additives.

1. Heat 1 tablespoon oil over medium-high heat in each of 2 separate large broiler-proof skillets.

2. Add 3 ounces Canadian bacon to each skillet and sauté until it just begins to turn brown, stirring frequently, approximately 4 minutes.

3. Divide vegetables, basil, oregano, pepper, and salt evenly and add to the 2 skillets. Sauté until tender, stirring frequently, approximately 5 minutes.

4. In 2 separate small bowls, beat 3 eggs each with 1 tablespoon of water each.

5. Lower heat to medium and pour 1 bowl of eggs into each skillet. Cook approximately 3 minutes until eggs are mostly set.

6. Preheat broiler. Add grated cheese to each skillet. Place each skillet under the broiler until eggs are cooked through and starting to brown on top, approximately 3 minutes.

PER SERVING | Calories: 280 | Fat: 19g | Protein: 22g | Sodium: 885mg | Fiber: 1g | Carbohydrates: 5g | Sugar: 3g

Peanutty Noodle Bowl

This crunchy, colorful dish is equally good served warm or cold. It makes for an easy take-along dish for a workday lunch.

INGREDIENTS | SERVES 2

2 teaspoons sesame oil, divided

¼ cup shelled peanuts

1 tablespoon peanut butter

⅛ teaspoon ground ginger

⅛ teaspoon ground red pepper

⅛ teaspoon sea salt

¼ teaspoon lemon juice

½ teaspoon pure maple syrup

⅛ teaspoon pure vanilla extract

1–2 tablespoons filtered water

10 snow pea pods

½ cup shredded carrots

1½ cups cooked rice noodles

1. Add 1 teaspoon oil, peanuts, peanut butter, ginger, pepper, salt, lemon juice, syrup, vanilla, and 1 tablespoon filtered water to a blender. Run until all ingredients are combined and peanuts are reduced to tiny chunks. Add a little more water to thin, if necessary.

2. Heat remaining oil in a large sauté pan over medium-high heat. Add snow pea pods and carrots; stir-fry quickly for 3–5 minutes. Remove from heat.

3. In a large bowl, toss peanut sauce with vegetables and noodles. Divide mixture into 2 bowls and serve.

PER SERVING | Calories: 359 | Fat: 18g | Protein: 9g | Sodium: 230mg | Fiber: 5g | Carbohydrates: 43g | Sugar: 5g

Ground Red Pepper

Ground red pepper is typically made with cayenne peppers, but some manufacturers will use alternative red peppers. True ground cayenne will be slightly hotter than its look-alikes. Feel free to use either type in any low-FODMAP recipe.

Rice Paper Veggie Wraps

You will impress your guests with these elegant Asian-inspired delicacies.
Serve them with Carrot Dip on the side (see recipe in Chapter 15).

INGREDIENTS | SERVES 4

1 tablespoon sesame oil

1 tablespoon gluten-free tamari

1 tablespoon natural peanut butter

1 teaspoon turbinado sugar

1 tablespoon freshly squeezed lemon juice

½ cup matchstick-cut carrots

½ cup seeded, matchstick-cut cucumber

½ cup matchstick-cut snow peas

½ cup alfalfa sprouts

4 rice wraps

1. In a small bowl, make dressing: Whisk together oil, tamari, peanut butter, sugar, and lemon juice.

2. Mix carrots, cucumber, snow peas, and sprouts in a medium bowl and toss with dressing.

3. Prepare wraps according to package directions. Fill each with ½ cup vegetable mixture; wrap, roll, and serve.

PER SERVING | Calories: 380 | Fat: 23g | Protein: 11g | Sodium: 800mg | Fiber: 5g | Carbohydrates: 38g | Sugar: 11g

What Is Tamari?

Tamari is a Japanese soy sauce. Unlike regular soy sauce, tamari contains little to no wheat. Therefore, it is usually gluten-free and appropriate for a low-FODMAP diet. You don't need to worry about any loss of flavor; in fact tamari, with its darker color, has a deeper flavor than regular soy sauce.

Rosemary Chicken Salad

Great for picnics and parties, this make-ahead recipe can be doubled or tripled to feed larger crowds. If not serving immediately, make extra dressing and toss it in just before plating.

INGREDIENTS | SERVES 4

¼ cup full-fat mayonnaise

2 tablespoons lactose-free plain yogurt

1 tablespoon red wine vinegar

1 teaspoon dried rosemary, crumbled

2 cups cubed grilled chicken

2 cups sliced, seedless grapes

¼ cup sliced almonds, toasted

1. In a small bowl, make dressing: Whisk together mayonnaise, yogurt, vinegar, and rosemary.

2. In a large bowl, combine dressing with chicken and grapes and toss until combined.

3. Sprinkle with almonds and serve.

PER SERVING | Calories: 320 | Fat: 17g | Protein: 26g | Sodium: 210mg | Fiber: 1g | Carbohydrates: 16g | Sugar: 12g

CHAPTER 8

Soups

Vegetable Stock

Stock is a great way to use up fresh vegetable leftovers. As long as they're low-FODMAP, feel free to experiment with different combinations. Stock can be stored for up to two days in the refrigerator or several months in the freezer.

INGREDIENTS | MAKES 7 CUPS

¼ cup extra-virgin olive oil

1 small yellow onion, peeled and quartered

4 garlic cloves, peeled and slightly smashed

½ cup diced zucchini

½ cup diced carrot

½ cup diced eggplant

½ cup diced cucumber

½ cup diced broccoli

½ cup diced green beans

8 cups water

1 teaspoon sea salt

¼ teaspoon freshly ground black pepper

Cooking with Garlic and Onions

Although garlic and onions are considered to be high-FODMAP foods, you can still benefit from their flavor in cooking. FODMAPs are not soluble in oil, so you can sauté garlic and onion in oil for a few minutes at the start of a recipe, then discard them. This allows for a flavor-infused oil without the concerns about the FODMAPs found in the actual garlic and onions.

1. Heat oil over medium-low heat in a large stockpot. Add the onion and garlic and sauté, stirring constantly, until softened and brown at edges. Remove and discard onion and garlic from pot, leaving oil.

2. Add remaining vegetables and sauté, stirring occasionally, about 8–10 minutes.

3. Add 8 cups filtered water, salt, and pepper. Bring to a boil, then lower heat and simmer for 3 hours, uncovered.

4. Allow stock to cool. Using a slotted spoon, remove and discard largest vegetable pieces. Using a mesh colander, over a large bowl, strain remaining vegetables and debris, and reserve stock.

5. Transfer stock to a container for refrigerator storage.

PER SERVING (1 CUP) | Calories: 52 | Fat: 4g | Protein: 1g | Sodium: 345mg | Fiber: 1g | Carbohydrates: 4g | Sugar: 2g

Basic Roast Chicken Stock

Let the flavors from your roast chicken—such as the pumpkin and spice flavors of Autumn's Roast Chicken (see recipe in Chapter 11)—add character to your stock. Stock can be stored for up to two days in the refrigerator or several months in the freezer.

INGREDIENTS | MAKES 6 CUPS

1 roast chicken carcass, skin, and leftovers

8 cups filtered water

1 teaspoon sea salt

1 teaspoon freshly ground black pepper

Store-Bought Stock and the Low-FODMAP Diet

You cannot beat the convenience of store-bought stock. However, you will need to be quite selective in the brand that you buy. Read ingredient labels carefully—you will need to choose brands that are onion- and garlic-free. You also should not buy brands that contain "dehydrated vegetable powder."

1. Place all chicken parts in a large stockpot.

2. Cover with water. Add salt and pepper. Bring just to a boil and then lower heat. Stirring occasionally, simmer for 3 hours uncovered.

3. Allow stock to cool. Remove and discard large chicken parts. Using a mesh colander over a large bowl, strain remaining chicken parts and debris, and reserve stock.

4. Transfer stock to a container for refrigerator storage.

PER SERVING (1 CUP) | Calories: 80 | Fat: 5g | Protein: 10g | Sodium: 465mg | Fiber: 0g | Carbohydrates: 0g | Sugar: 0g

Seafood Stock

When making the Shrimp with Cherry Tomatoes or Coconut Shrimp (see recipes in Chapter 12), save the shells to make this stock. It freezes well, so you'll always have this low-FODMAP "pantry" essential on hand.

INGREDIENTS | MAKES 6 CUPS

2 tablespoons extra-virgin olive oil

2 garlic cloves, peeled and slightly crushed

1 medium yellow onion, peeled and quartered

2 large carrots, peeled and diced

1 medium zucchini, trimmed and diced

12 large raw shrimp shells

6 cups water

½ cup Tomato Paste (see recipe in Chapter 9)

½ cup dry white wine

1 tablespoon sea salt

1 teaspoon freshly ground black pepper

Cooking with Wine

Although both drinking wine and cooking wines are permitted on the low-FODMAP diet, keep in mind that cooking wines sold in the supermarket typically have high sodium levels that may affect the flavor of the dish. You can save your leftover drinking wine in ice cube trays in the freezer for up to three months for later use.

1. Heat oil over medium-low heat in a large skillet. Add the garlic and onion and sauté, stirring constantly, until garlic is softened and brown at edges, about 5 minutes. Remove and discard garlic and onion, leaving oil.

2. Increase heat to medium-high, add carrots and zucchini, and sauté 5 minutes.

3. Add shrimp shells, 6 cups water, tomato paste, wine, salt, and pepper and stir until paste is completely dissolved.

4. Bring just to a boil, then reduce heat to low and simmer for 45 minutes, uncovered.

5. Remove from heat and allow stock to cool. Using a slotted spoon, remove and discard shells and large debris. Using a mesh colander over a large bowl, strain remaining solids and reserve stock.

6. Transfer stock to a container for refrigerator storage.

PER SERVING (1 CUP) | Calories: 100 | Fat: 6g | Protein: 1g | Sodium: 1,400mg | Fiber: 2g | Carbohydrates: 8g | Sugar: 4g

Acorn Squash and Chard Soup

You will enjoy many of the colors of the rainbow as you prepare this soothing soup. Throw the squash in the oven before you start prepping the other ingredients. This will give it time to cool before you need it to finish the soup. Skip the Canadian bacon for a delicious vegetarian option.

INGREDIENTS | SERVES 4

2 medium acorn squash

2 tablespoons extra-virgin olive oil, divided

1 (6-ounce) package Canadian bacon, diced

1 bunch Swiss chard, stems removed, chopped roughly

3 cups filtered water

1 teaspoon ground turmeric

1 teaspoon ground cinnamon

¼ teaspoon freshly ground black pepper

Get to Know Turmeric

Turmeric is a gorgeous yellow spice that has been used for centuries as a medicine in traditional cultures and is now sold in supplement form. Research shows that turmeric has strong anti-inflammatory qualities and may help with cancer prevention. Turmeric can stain things yellow, so be cautious with what it touches in your kitchen.

1. Heat oven to 400°F. Roast whole squash on a rimmed baking sheet for 1 hour until tender, turning occasionally. Remove from heat and cool for 30 minutes.

2. While squash is cooking, heat 1 tablespoon olive oil over medium heat in a stockpot. Sauté Canadian bacon, stirring occasionally, 8 minutes until browned. Remove from pan using a slotted spoon, leaving drippings in pan, and place on a paper towel–lined plate to dry.

3. Add remaining olive oil to pot. Sauté Swiss chard for 3 minutes, stirring occasionally until wilted.

4. Once squash has cooled, cut each one in half lengthwise. Scoop out seeds and discard. Scoop cooked flesh from skin and process in a blender or food processor until smooth.

5. Add puréed squash to soup pot with the chard. Add 3 cups filtered water, turmeric, cinnamon, and pepper. Simmer 5 minutes, uncovered. Remove from heat.

6. Serve with Canadian bacon as garnish.

PER SERVING | Calories: 222 | Fat: 10g | Protein: 11g | Sodium: 675mg | Fiber: 4g | Carbohydrates: 25g | Sugar: 0g

Roasted Vegetable Soup

Make this warm and satisfying soup any time you need a little extra nurturing. You can substitute the Vegetable Stock found in this chapter to make it appropriate for a vegetarian diet.

INGREDIENTS | SERVES 8

1 recipe Roasted Vegetables (see recipe in Chapter 13)

1 (14.5-ounce) can diced tomatoes

6 cups Basic Roast Chicken Stock (see recipe in this chapter)

1 tablespoon chopped fresh flat-leaf parsley

1. Place vegetables in a stockpot and add tomatoes and stock. Stir to combine. Working in batches, place vegetables in a blender or food processor. Blend until smooth. If desired, you can leave some vegetables unblended for texture.

2. Return puréed vegetables to pot. Heat on high until boiling. Lower heat and simmer, uncovered, for 20 minutes to blend flavors and heat through.

3. Serve with a garnish of chopped parsley.

PER SERVING | Calories: 270 | Fat: 10g | Protein: 12g | Sodium: 545mg | Fiber: 11g | Carbohydrates: 34g | Sugar: 11g

Red Pepper Soup

Surprisingly, a few drops of vanilla enhance the savory flavors of this delightful soup. Serve it warm in winter—sans the toppings—or cool, as described, in the summer months.

INGREDIENTS | SERVES 6

1 tablespoon extra-virgin olive oil

3 medium red bell peppers, seeded and diced

1 large red potato, peeled and diced

1 cup diced carrot

1 large parsnip, peeled and diced

6 cups water

¼ teaspoon sea salt

⅛ teaspoon freshly ground black pepper

⅛ teaspoon pure vanilla extract

¾ cup coconut milk, refrigerated

¼ cup chopped fresh chives, divided

1. Heat oil over medium-low heat in a large stockpot.

2. Add vegetables and sauté for 10 minutes. Add 6 cups of water. Bring to a boil, lower heat, and simmer uncovered 2–3 hours, until vegetables are very tender. Season with salt and pepper. Stir in vanilla. Remove from heat and cool completely.

3. Once cool, purée soup in batches in a food processor or blender.

4. Fill 6 individual serving bowls with 1 cup of soup each. Swirl in 2 tablespoons coconut milk and sprinkle with a heaping ½ tablespoon chives.

PER SERVING | Calories: 125 | Fat: 6g | Protein: 2g | Sodium: 120mg | Fiber: 4g | Carbohydrates: 16g | Sugar: 5g

Bean-Free Minestrone

You will certainly get your daily veggies with this colorful soup. The cheese rind is added for flavor and texture and then removed before serving.

INGREDIENTS | SERVES 6

1 medium eggplant

1 tablespoon Garlic-Infused Oil (see recipe in Chapter 9)

1 cup sliced baby carrots

1 medium zucchini, diced

1 (28-ounce) can crushed tomatoes

1 (14.5-ounce) can diced tomatoes

¼ teaspoon sea salt

¼ teaspoon freshly ground black pepper

5 cups filtered water

1 (1" × 3") Parmesan cheese rind

6-ounce box gluten-free elbow pasta

1. Slice eggplant lengthwise and remove inside flesh (save for Gingerbread Cupcakes recipe in Chapter 14, if desired). Cut the outer edges (skin) of the eggplant into 1" cubes.

2. In a large stockpot, heat oil over medium-high heat. Add eggplant and sauté for 15 minutes. Add carrots and zucchini and sauté 10 minutes more.

3. Add tomatoes, salt, pepper, and 5 cups filtered water. Bring just to a boil, then lower heat, add rind, and simmer uncovered for 30 minutes. Add pasta and simmer uncovered 10 minutes more.

4. Remove and discard remainder of cheese rind and serve.

PER SERVING | Calories: 195 | Fat: 3g | Protein: 7g | Sodium: 410mg | Fiber: 7g | Carbohydrates: 38g | Sugar: 10g

Forbidden Rice Chicken Soup

This recipe calls for black forbidden rice—which adds drama and a nutty flavor—but any brown or white rice may be substituted. You will be getting plenty of super-healthy phytonutrients from the colorful vegetables that make up this nutritious soup.

INGREDIENTS | SERVES 6

1 teaspoon sesame oil

1 medium sweet yellow onion, peeled and quartered

2 garlic cloves, peeled, slightly smashed

1½ cups peeled and cubed butternut squash

3 cups Basic Roast Chicken Stock (see recipe in this chapter)

Filtered water (amount will vary)

1½ cups chopped green beans

1 teaspoon sea salt

½ teaspoon freshly ground black pepper

6 ounces cooked, skinless, boneless chicken breast, shredded

1 cup packed baby spinach leaves

3 cups cooked forbidden rice

1. Swirl oil in large stockpot over medium heat.

2. Add onion and garlic and stir until fragrant, about 2–3 minutes. Remove and discard onion and garlic.

3. Add squash and sauté 5 minutes. Add stock and enough filtered water to cover squash. Bring just to a boil, then lower heat. Simmer uncovered 20 minutes.

4. Add green beans, salt, and pepper and stir. Simmer uncovered 10 minutes more. Add chicken and spinach and stir just until greens are wilted.

5. Fill each soup bowl with ½ cup rice. Ladle a generous cup of soup over rice.

6. Per Serving | Calories: 220 | Fat: 5g | Protein: 21g | Sodium: 525mg | Fiber: 4g | Carbohydrates: 26g | Sugar: 3g

Butternut Squash and the Low-FODMAP Diet

Butternut squash does contain some GOS and mannitol. You should be safe if you keep your serving size to no more than ¼ cup diced. Like all colorful fruits and vegetables, butternut squash is filled with lots of antioxidants and phytochemicals and so is definitely worth including in your diet.

Shrimp Bisque

The elegance of this easy soup will make a regular mealtime feel like a special occasion. You also have the option of serving this soup as the first course of your next dinner party.

INGREDIENTS | SERVES 6

1 tablespoon extra-virgin olive oil

4 medium carrots, peeled and sliced into ¼" rounds

1 medium red bell pepper, seeded and diced

4 cups Basic Roast Chicken Stock (see recipe in this chapter)

1 (14.5-ounce) can diced tomatoes

1½ pounds uncooked shrimp, peeled and deveined

½ cup lactose-free milk

¼ cup white wine

1 pinch crushed red pepper

2 tablespoons chopped fresh flat-leaf parsley

1. Heat olive oil in a stockpot over medium-high heat. Add carrots and red bell pepper and sauté for 5 minutes.

2. Add stock and tomatoes. Bring to a boil, then lower heat and simmer, uncovered, for 15 minutes.

3. As soup is simmering, divide shrimp into 2 piles and set 1 pile aside. Take the remaining shrimp and cut each into thirds.

4. Once the soup has simmered for 15 minutes, add the whole shrimp to the pot. Cook for 5 minutes until shrimp is cooked through.

5. Pour contents of stockpot into a blender, working in batches if necessary. Blend until smooth.

6. Return soup to pot. Add milk, wine, and crushed red pepper. Simmer uncovered for 2 minutes.

7. Add chopped shrimp to pot and cook through, 5 minutes. Serve soup with a garnish of parsley.

PER SERVING | Calories: 175 | Fat: 7g | Protein: 30g | Sodium: 405mg | Fiber: 3g | Carbohydrates: 11g | Sugar: 6g

Turkey and Brown Rice Soup

This soup, packed with colorful vegetables, is sure to be a crowd pleaser. Alternately, you can divide it up and freeze it for a quick, warming lunch option.

INGREDIENTS | SERVES 6

1 cup brown rice, rinsed

2 tablespoons extra-virgin olive oil

4 medium carrots, peeled and sliced into ¼" rounds

1 medium red bell pepper, seeded and diced

1 bay leaf

6 cups Basic Roast Chicken Stock (see recipe in this chapter)

1 (14.5-ounce) can of diced tomatoes

4 (3-ounce) turkey breast cutlets (uncooked), cut into 1" squares

5 cups baby spinach leaves

2 tablespoons chopped fresh flat-leaf parsley

⅛ teaspoon sea salt

⅛ teaspoon freshly ground black pepper

1. Cook rice in a saucepan or rice cooker according to package directions.

2. Heat olive oil in a stockpot over medium-high heat. Add carrots, bell pepper, and bay leaf. Sauté 5 minutes, stirring occasionally.

3. Add stock, tomatoes, and turkey to soup pot. Bring to a boil, then turn down heat and simmer, uncovered, for 45 minutes, stirring occasionally.

4. Remove bay leaf and stir in spinach until wilted.

5. Turn off heat. Stir in rice, parsley, salt, and pepper.

PER SERVING | Calories: 345 | Fat: 9g | Protein: 28g | Sodium: 325mg | Fiber: 4g | Carbohydrates: 33g | Sugar: 5g

Should Rice Be Rinsed?

This is one of the many food preparation questions that seem to be up for debate. The best answer is that it depends on how you like your rice. Rinsing your rice rids it of surface starches, which helps prevent clumps. If the recipe calls for a stickier rice, such as one would see in risotto or sticky rice for sushi, you would not rinse your rice before cooking it.

Carrot and Ginger Soup

This elegant soup is sure to be soothing to your whole system. Feel free to substitute Vegetable Stock (see recipe in this chapter) for a vegetarian version.

INGREDIENTS | SERVES 6

2 tablespoons pumpkin seeds

2 tablespoons extra-virgin olive oil

1 pound carrots, peeled and thinly sliced

1 (2-inch) piece of ginger, peeled and grated

4 cups Basic Roast Chicken Stock (see recipe in this chapter)

¼ cup freshly squeezed orange juice (1 whole orange)

2 teaspoons grated orange zest

⅛ teaspoon sea salt

⅛ teaspoon freshly ground black pepper

1. Toast pumpkin seeds on a rimmed baking sheet under broiler for 3 minutes. Set aside.

2. Heat oil in a large stockpot over medium-low heat. Add carrots and ginger and sauté for 5 minutes, stirring frequently.

3. Add stock. Turn heat to high and bring just to a boil, then lower heat and simmer, uncovered, for 20 minutes until carrots are soft.

4. Purée the soup in a blender or food processor. Return to pot.

5. Stir in orange juice, zest, salt, and pepper.

6. Serve soup in bowls garnished with pumpkin seeds.

PER SERVING | Calories: 185 | Fat: 8g | Protein: 9g | Sodium: 175mg | Fiber: 3g | Carbohydrates: 33g | Sugar: 5g

Sauces, Dressings, and Rubs

Tomato Purée

Due to the concern about excessive fructose in canned tomato purée, it is a good idea to make your own. This is a basic recipe, but feel free to experiment with FODMAP-friendly seasonings, such as basil, oregano, or parsley. You can double or triple this recipe and store it in batches in the freezer for several months.

INGREDIENTS | MAKES 1½ CUPS

1 tablespoon Garlic-Infused Oil (see recipe in this chapter)

5 medium ripe tomatoes, cored, seeded, and diced

1 teaspoon sea salt

¼ teaspoon freshly ground black pepper

Canned Tomatoes and the Low-FODMAP Diet

Although tomatoes are allowed on the low-FODMAP diet, this does not mean that all tomato products are okay. Canned tomato paste and purée may have excessive levels of fructose. It is best to use fresh tomatoes or canned tomatoes with thin, watery juice.

1. Heat oil over medium-low heat in a large saucepan. Add tomatoes to oil and stir. Season with salt and pepper. Sauté, stirring occasionally, for 15–20 minutes, until tomatoes are soft and broken down. Remove from heat to cool.

2. Transfer cooled tomatoes to a food processor and blend completely. Set a large strainer over a large bowl. Transfer purée to strainer. Press down with a large spoon to completely separate solids in strainer from purée in bowl.

3. Transfer to an airtight container and store in the refrigerator.

PER SERVING (½ CUP) | Calories: 77 | Fat: 5g | Protein: 2g | Sodium: 795mg | Fiber: 3g | Carbohydrates: 8g | Sugar: 5g

Tomato Paste

Tomato paste is a pantry staple—used to thicken and flavor many tomato-based recipes. Store in an airtight container in the refrigerator for up to three days, or in the freezer for several months.

INGREDIENTS | MAKES ⅓ CUP

1½ cups Tomato Purée (see recipe in this chapter)

1. Preheat oven to 300°F. Pour purée into an ovenproof skillet.

2. Cook, uncovered, for about 2 hours, stirring every 20 minutes, until a paste consistency is formed.

3. Cool completely.

PER SERVING (1 TABLESPOON) | Calories: 22 | Fat: 0g | Protein: 1g | Sodium: 475mg | Fiber: 1g | Carbohydrates: 5g | Sugar: 3g

Roasted Tomato Sauce

This sauce makes a lovely summer supper served over gluten-free pasta. The more varieties of fresh, colorful tomatoes you use, the prettier this sauce gets.

INGREDIENTS | MAKES 2 CUPS

2 tablespoons Garlic-Infused Oil (see recipe in this chapter)

1 teaspoon salt

1½ pounds fresh tomatoes, cored, seeded and diced

1 bay leaf

⅛ teaspoon crushed red pepper

1. Preheat oven to 400°F. Line a roasting pan with parchment paper.

2. Place all ingredients in a medium bowl and toss to thoroughly combine. Transfer to roasting pan and spread tomatoes in one thin layer.

3. Roast for 20 minutes, tossing halfway through. Remove and discard bay leaf. Transfer to a bowl and stir.

PER SERVING (½ CUP) | Calories: 90 | Fat: 7g | Protein: 1g | Sodium: 600mg | Fiber: 2g | Carbohydrates: 7g | Sugar: 4g

Traditional Tomato Sauce

Most bottled tomato sauces include garlic or onions, so it's best to make your own. It takes some time—but this recipe freezes well. It's a rustic, chunky style. For a smoother consistency, simply cool the sauce and purée before serving.

INGREDIENTS | MAKES 6 CUPS

¼ cup extra-virgin olive oil

1 medium onion, peeled and quartered

4 garlic cloves, peeled and slightly smashed

1½ cups Tomato Purée (see recipe in this chapter)

1 (14-ounce) can San Marzano diced tomatoes

1 (14-ounce) can whole peeled San Marzano tomatoes

1 teaspoon dried oregano

1 teaspoon dried basil

1 tablespoon turbinado sugar

1 (1" × 3") Parmesan cheese rind

1. Heat oil over medium-low heat in a large saucepan. Add the onion and garlic and sauté, stirring constantly, until garlic is softened and brown at edges. Remove and discard onion and garlic, leaving oil.

2. Add remaining ingredients, except for cheese rind; stir to combine. Break up whole tomatoes with a pair of kitchen shears.

3. Bring just to a boil, then reduce heat to low. Add cheese rind and simmer uncovered, stirring occasionally, for 1½–2 hours. Remove remainder of rind before serving.

PER SERVING (1 CUP) | Calories: 180 | Fat: 12g | Protein: 3g | Sodium: 825mg | Fiber: 4g | Carbohydrates: 19g | Sugar: 12g

San Marzano Tomatoes

San Marzano is a variety of tomato, not a brand name. Unlike regular round tomatoes, their appearance is long and thin. The tomatoes are naturally sweeter than others, so there is no need to add a lot of extra sugar to your sauce.

Alfredo Sauce

Using this classic sauce as a base, you can make a variety of different meals. Try gluten-free rigatoni with cubes of grilled chicken, roasted red peppers, a sprinkle of freshly cooked corn, and basil.

INGREDIENTS | MAKES 1½ CUPS

1 tablespoon butter

4 garlic cloves, peeled, slightly smashed

1 tablespoon sweet rice flour

1⅓ cups lactose-free milk

1 teaspoon sea salt

¼ teaspoon freshly ground black pepper

1 cup grated Parmesan cheese

½ cup Whipped Cream (see recipe in Chapter 14)

Whipped Cream and the Low-FODMAP Diet

Because most milk-based products are not allowed on the low-FODMAP diet, it may surprise you to see whipped cream on the allowed list. This is because the amount of air in the product keeps the overall lactose level low. The serving size limit is 2 tablespoons.

1. Heat butter over medium-low heat in a medium saucepan. Add the garlic and sauté, stirring constantly, until softened and brown at edges. Remove and discard garlic, leaving butter.

2. Add flour and whisk constantly for 1–2 minutes until thickened and light golden brown.

3. Slowly whisk in milk. Cook, whisking constantly, until thickened and bubbling, about 8–10 minutes. Remove from heat, season with salt and pepper, and stir in cheese.

4. Fold in whipped cream and serve.

PER SERVING (½ CUP) | Calories: 330 | Fat: 24g | Protein: 17g | Sodium: 1,350mg | Fiber: 0g | Carbohydrates: 11g | Sugar: 6g

Bolognese Sauce

Serve this rich, indulgent sauce over your favorite gluten-free pasta. It's perfect for a warming weekday meal or an elegant dinner party.

INGREDIENTS | SERVES 8

2 tablespoons extra-virgin olive oil

2 tablespoons butter

1 medium yellow onion, peeled and quartered

2 garlic cloves, peeled, slightly smashed

1½ cups finely diced carrots

1 pound ground meatball mix (beef, pork, and veal)

½ cup dry white wine

1 teaspoon sea salt

⅛ teaspoon freshly ground black pepper

⅛ teaspoon ground nutmeg

1 (14.5-ounce) can diced fire-roasted tomatoes

1 tablespoon Tomato Paste (see recipe in this chapter)

1 (1" × 3") Parmesan cheese rind

½ cup Whipped Cream (see recipe in Chapter 14)

1. Heat oil and butter over medium-low heat in a large stockpot. Add the onion and garlic and sauté, stirring constantly, until garlic is softened and brown at edges. Remove and discard onion and garlic, leaving oil and butter.

2. Add carrots to oil and sauté over medium-low heat for 15 minutes, stirring occasionally.

3. Add meat and cook, stirring often to break up into bits, for about 10–15 minutes or until meat is fully browned.

4. Add wine and simmer uncovered 10 minutes.

5. Add salt, pepper, nutmeg, tomatoes, paste, and rind, and simmer uncovered 1½–2 hours more, stirring occasionally.

6. Remove rind, fold in whipped cream, and serve.

PER SERVING | Calories: 210 | Fat: 14g | Protein: 12g | Sodium: 415mg | Fiber: 1g | Carbohydrates: 6g | Sugar: 3g

Cheese Rinds

You no longer need to throw away hard cheese rinds, such as Parmesan or pecorino. When added to soups and sauces they soften and then suffuse their cheesy goodness into the liquid. You can store any leftovers in the freezer until you're ready to use them. Be sure to remove what is left of the rind prior to serving the dish.

Sun-Dried Tomato Pesto

The low-FODMAP diet allows for two pieces of sun-dried tomatoes per serving.
The use of spinach in this pesto enables that small amount to go a long way.
Serve over gluten-free pasta or as a dip with gluten-free crackers.

INGREDIENTS | MAKES ⅓ CUP

2 tablespoons walnut oil

¼ cup walnuts, toasted

¼ cup sun-dried tomatoes

1 cup packed baby spinach leaves

½ teaspoon sea salt

¼ cup freshly grated Parmesan cheese

Add all ingredients to a food processor and blend to a pesto consistency.

PER SERVING (2 TABLESPOONS) | Calories: 290 | Fat: 27g | Protein: 9g | Sodium: 670mg | Fiber: 2g | Carbohydrates: 7g | Sugar: 3g

Garden Pesto

Most pestos rely on garlic as a main ingredient. This recipe captures its flavor, but saves your tummy the trouble of trying to digest it.

INGREDIENTS | MAKES ⅓ CUP

2 tablespoons Garlic-Infused Oil (see recipe in this chapter)

¼ cup pine nuts, toasted

1 cup packed basil leaves

½ teaspoon sea salt

¼ cup freshly grated Parmesan cheese

Add all ingredients to a food processor and blend to a pesto consistency.

PER SERVING (2 TABLESPOONS) | Calories: 178 | Fat: 17g | Protein: 5g | Sodium: 350mg | Fiber: 1g | Carbohydrates: 2g | Sugar: 0g

Garlic-Infused Oil

Serve this luscious homemade oil as a dip alongside a crusty gluten-free bread or use in your weeknight recipes. As with all homemade bottled goods, to safeguard against botulism, store leftovers in an airtight container in the refrigerator for up to one week.

INGREDIENTS | MAKES 1 CUP

1 cup plus 1 teaspoon grapeseed oil
4 garlic cloves, peeled, slightly smashed

Heat oil in a small saucepan over medium-low heat, add garlic, and sauté for 10 minutes, stirring often. Remove from heat and allow to completely cool. Remove and discard garlic, reserving oil.

PER SERVING (1 TABLESPOON) | Calories: 123 | Fat: 14g | Protein: 0g | Sodium: 0mg | Fiber: 0g | Carbohydrates: 0g | Sugar: 0g

Italian Vegetable Sauce

You will love all of the colors in your stockpot—everyone else will love how delicious all these vegetables taste! Serve over your favorite gluten-free pasta.

INGREDIENTS | MAKES 6 CUPS

2 tablespoons extra-virgin olive oil

2 medium red bell peppers, seeded and diced

2 medium green bell peppers, seeded and diced

4 large carrots, peeled and cut into thin rounds

2 medium zucchini, quartered lengthwise and cut into ¼" slices

1 (28-ounce) can whole tomatoes

2 tablespoons demerara sugar

1 tablespoon dried basil

1 tablespoon dried oregano

½ teaspoon ground cinnamon

½ teaspoon ground dried ginger

1 pinch crushed red pepper

⅛ teaspoon sea salt

⅛ teaspoon freshly ground black pepper

1. Heat olive oil in a large stockpot over medium-high heat. Add bell peppers, carrots, and zucchini to pot and sauté until crisp-tender, approximately 10 minutes, stirring frequently.

2. Add tomatoes (breaking them up with your hands), sugar, basil, oregano, cinnamon, ginger, crushed red pepper, salt, and black pepper. Bring to a boil, then simmer, uncovered, for 60 minutes.

PER SERVING (1 CUP) | Calories: 130 | Fat: 5g | Protein: 3g | Sodium: 275mg | Fiber: 5g | Carbohydrates: 21g | Sugar: 14g

Pepperonata Sauce

With its colorful array of sweet bell peppers, this versatile sauce brightens up pasta, sandwiches, even grilled meats and fish.

2 tablespoons Garlic-Infused Oil (see recipe in this chapter)

12 medium red, yellow, and green bell peppers, seeded and diced

1 tablespoon balsamic vinegar

⅛ teaspoon sea salt

⅛ teaspoon freshly ground pepper

Balsamic Vinegar and the Low-FODMAP Diet

In larger quantities, balsamic vinegar can contain excess fructose, making it inappropriate for a low-FODMAP diet. Keeping your serving size to no more than 1 tablespoon ensures an optimal fructose/glucose balance—low enough for all phases of the diet.

1. Heat oil over medium heat in a large stockpot. Add peppers and sauté 5 minutes. Add vinegar, salt, and pepper and stir.

2. Reduce heat and simmer uncovered for 1½–2 hours, stirring occasionally, until peppers are fork tender.

PER SERVING (1 CUP) | Calories: 87 | Fat: 4g | Protein: 2g | Sodium: 45mg | Fiber: 4g | Carbohydrates: 11g | Sugar: 8g

Scampi Primavera Sauce

Pair this versatile, veggie-packed sauce with grilled, broiled, or sautéed shrimp or any type of white fish over gluten-free spaghetti.

INGREDIENTS | MAKES 2½ CUPS

1 teaspoon grated lemon zest

1 tablespoon lemon juice

½ cup dry white wine

1 cup Vegetable Stock (see recipe in Chapter 8)

½ teaspoon sea salt

¼ teaspoon freshly ground black pepper

1 medium red bell pepper, seeded and finely diced

1 medium carrot, peeled and finely diced

1 cup finely diced green beans

1 medium tomato, cored, seeded, and finely diced

1 small zucchini, seeded and finely diced

1 tablespoon butter

1 garlic clove, peeled and slightly crushed

1 tablespoon sweet rice flour

¼ cup Parmesan cheese

1 tablespoon chopped parsley

1. In a medium bowl, mix lemon zest, juice, wine, stock, salt, and pepper. Stir in bell pepper, carrot, green beans, tomato, and zucchini. Set aside.

2. Heat butter over medium-low heat in a medium saucepan. Add the garlic and sauté, stirring constantly, until softened and brown at edges, about 5 minutes. Remove and discard garlic, leaving butter.

3. Add flour and whisk constantly for 1–2 minutes until thickened and light golden brown. Increase heat to medium-high. Add vegetable mixture and liquid from bowl and stir well. Bring just to a boil.

4. Reduce heat to medium-low and simmer uncovered, stirring occasionally, until sauce thickens and vegetables are tender. Sprinkle with Parmesan and parsley prior to serving.

PER SERVING (½ CUP) | Calories: 105 | Fat: 4g | Protein: 4g | Sodium: 450mg | Fiber: 2g | Carbohydrates: 10g | Sugar: 5g

Your Five or More for the Day

One of the greatest things about the low-FODMAP diet is that you can now eat vegetables and fruit with confidence, rather than anxiety. Try to make it a point to eat some produce with every meal. Be creative and have fun figuring out where you can add extra low-FODMAP vegetables to your favorite recipes.

Sweet Barbecue Sauce

Specialty items, such as smoked sea salt, smoked paprika, piloncillo (a sugar with a slightly smoky flavor), and bacon, can be purchased and subbed in for their recipe counterparts to suit a preference for smokier barbecue sauce flavor.

INGREDIENTS | MAKES 1 CUP

1 cup Tomato Purée (see recipe in this chapter)

1 tablespoon Dijon mustard

1 tablespoon blackstrap molasses

1½ tablespoons pure maple syrup

½ teaspoon ground cinnamon

½ teaspoon ground cumin

½ teaspoon dried oregano

½ teaspoon white wine vinegar

½ teaspoon arrowroot powder

½ teaspoon paprika

⅛ teaspoon ground red pepper

⅛ teaspoon nutmeg

⅛ teaspoon sea salt

Bring all ingredients just to a boil in a small saucepan over medium-high heat. Lower heat and simmer, uncovered, 5–10 minutes, or until sauce thickens.

PER SERVING (2 TABLESPOONS) | Calories: 25 | Fat: 0g | Protein: 1g | Sodium: 100mg | Fiber: 1g | Carbohydrates: 6g | Sugar: 5g

Barbecue Sauce and the Low-FODMAP Diet

Most, if not all, of the barbecue sauces you will find on the shelves at your local supermarket are filled with high-FODMAP ingredients, such as high fructose corn syrup (HFCS), onions, and garlic. To continue to enjoy the traditional taste of barbecue sauce, you will need to make your own.

Artisanal Ketchup

The best thing about making your own ketchup is that you can flavor it to suit your dishes and taste preferences. This recipe features a sweet and savory spice blend, but you can substitute thyme and bay leaf for the spices in this recipe to achieve a woodsier effect.

INGREDIENTS | MAKES ¾ CUP

¾ cup Tomato Paste (see recipe in this chapter)

1 tablespoon white wine vinegar

1 tablespoon Simple Brown Syrup (see recipe in Chapter 16)

¼ teaspoon dried oregano

⅛ teaspoon ground cumin

⅛ teaspoon ground cinnamon

Water (as needed)

Blend all ingredients in a food processor, adding water ¼ cup at a time, until desired consistency is achieved.

PER SERVING (2 TABLESPOONS) | Calories: 53 | Fat: 2g | Protein: 1g | Sodium: 55mg | Fiber: 1g | Carbohydrates: 8g | Sugar: 6g

Ketchup and the Low-FODMAP Diet

Unfortunately, the convenience of super-market ketchup cannot be enjoyed on the low-FODMAP diet, as most of the major brands are made with HFCS and garlic and onion powder. You will need to make your own to ensure you are only eating appropriate ingredients. Be sure to take some along with you on road trips or for barbecues or sporting events.

Steakhouse Rub

You need not worry about any FODMAP carbohydrates when eating animal protein. Sprinkle and rub this savory mixture of herbs and spices into your favorite cut of beef before grilling.

INGREDIENTS | SERVES 4

1 teaspoon sea salt

¼ teaspoon freshly ground black pepper

¼ teaspoon ground mustard

½ teaspoon dried thyme

½ teaspoon dried rosemary, crumbled

¼ teaspoon maple sugar

½ teaspoon orange zest

Combine all ingredients in a small bowl.

PER SERVING | Calories: 2 | Fat: 0g | Protein: 0g | Sodium: 590mg | Fiber: 0g | Carbohydrates: 0g | Sugar: 0g

What Is Orange Zest?

Orange zest is made up of thin strips of the outer peel of an orange. It does not include any of the white pith, which has a more bitter taste. If you don't have a zester, you can use a regular grater.

Pork Loin Rub

*This easy-to-make-ahead seasoning can be rubbed on all sides of
a 1–2 pound boneless pork loin before grilling.*

INGREDIENTS | MAKES ⅓ CUP

1 tablespoon sea salt

1 tablespoon demerara sugar

1 tablespoon ground cinnamon

1 tablespoon sweet paprika

1 teaspoon dried oregano

½ teaspoon ground cumin

½ teaspoon ground red pepper

Mix all ingredients together in a small bowl.

PER SERVING (1 TABLESPOON) | Calories: 19 | Fat: 0g |
Protein: 0g | Sodium: 1,410mg | Fiber: 1g | Carbohydrates: 5g |
Sugar: 3g

Autumn's Glaze

It doesn't have to be fall for you to dazzle your family or guests as you dress up your carved roast chicken with this fast, delicious autumnal glaze.

INGREDIENTS | SERVES 4

2 tablespoons butter
¼ cup hulled pumpkin seeds
⅛ teaspoon sea salt
3 tablespoons pure maple syrup, divided
1 tablespoon Dijon mustard

1. Melt butter in a small saucepan and set aside.

2. Preheat broiler. Spread pumpkin seeds on a lined baking sheet. Drizzle 1 tablespoon of melted butter over pumpkin seeds. Sprinkle on salt. Toss seeds to coat. Broil for 1–2 minutes, or until seeds start to brown lightly. Remove from oven. Move seeds to serving dish and mix in 1 tablespoon maple syrup.

3. Return saucepan that contains the remaining tablespoon of butter to cooktop. Over medium heat, add remaining maple syrup and mustard. Bring just to a boil, then lower heat and simmer, uncovered, 1–2 minutes more to thicken.

4. The glaze and roasted seeds can be used to top any roasted poultry.

PER SERVING | Calories: 140 | Fat: 10g | Protein: 3g | Sodium: 120mg | Fiber: 1g | Carbohydrates: 11g | Sugar: 9g

Maple Mustard Dipping Sauce

The kids never need to know about the fact that you are serving them FODMAP-friendly foods. Serve this tangy dip alongside Caramel Oat Chicken Fingers (see recipe in Chapter 11).

INGREDIENTS | SERVES 4

1 tablespoon light sour cream

1 tablespoon pure maple syrup

1 tablespoon Dijon mustard

Whisk together all ingredients in a small bowl and serve.

PER SERVING | Calories: 20 | Fat: 0g | Protein: 0g | Sodium: 45mg | Fiber: 0g | Carbohydrates: 4g | Sugar: 3g

Tzatziki Dressing

This smooth dressing can be drizzled over grilled meats, fish, or salads. It captures the flavors and nutrients of traditional tzatziki sauce. Even garlic plays a role via infused oil.

INGREDIENTS | MAKES 1 CUP

½ cucumber, seeded and diced

½ cup lactose-free plain yogurt

1 teaspoon Garlic-Infused Oil (see recipe in this chapter)

1 tablespoon freshly squeezed lemon juice

1 tablespoon fresh dill

Place all ingredients in a blender and process until smooth.

PER SERVING (2 TABLESPOONS) | Calories: 18 | Fat: 1g | Protein: 1g | Sodium: 11mg | Fiber: 0g | Carbohydrates: 2g | Sugar: 1g

Kiwi Dipping Sauce

This sweet sauce with its hint of tang pairs beautifully with Coconut Shrimp (see recipe in Chapter 12), but you could also serve it atop slices of Brie on gluten-free crackers. For a prettier shade of green, cut around the kiwi's seeds, using only seed-free pieces for the dip.

INGREDIENTS | SERVES 4

½ cup peeled, chopped, seeded kiwi

½ cup peeled, cored, chopped pineapple

½ teaspoon freshly grated ginger

⅛ teaspoon pure vanilla extract

½ teaspoon fresh lime juice

Process all ingredients in a blender and serve.

PER SERVING | Calories: 45 | Fat: 0g | Protein: 1g | Sodium: 3mg | Fiber: 2g | Carbohydrates: 11g | Sugar: 2g

Kiwi for Health

It would be beneficial for you to add kiwi to your regular diet. Kiwi is a good source of vitamins C and K, as well as fiber, potassium, and a whole host of phytonutrients and antioxidants. As a bonus, kiwi has a positive effect on stool formation and may help to ease constipation.

CHAPTER 10

Pasta

Broccoli and Bow Ties

This recipe is a good one for getting vegetables into little kids—you can call it butterfly pasta if you like. If you can't find gluten-free farfalle, feel free to substitute any gluten-free pasta.

INGREDIENTS | SERVES 4

9 ounces gluten-free farfalle

2 cups chopped broccoli florets

1 cup frozen peas, thawed

1 tablespoon Garlic-Infused Oil (see recipe in Chapter 9)

1 (28-ounce) can whole tomatoes

1 tablespoon dried oregano

1 tablespoon dried basil

⅛ teaspoon freshly ground black pepper

Gluten-Free Pasta

The fact that you now have so many gluten-free options makes following the low-FODMAP diet so much easier! Gluten-free pasta options include those made with brown rice, corn, and quinoa. Be sure to read recipe ingredients to be assured there are no high-FODMAP foods lurking, such as soy or chickpeas. Although chickpeas are allowed in a ¼ cup portion size, you may not be able assess how many were used to create the pasta product.

1. Cook pasta according to package directions.

2. Fill a large saucepot with water and bring to a boil over high heat. Add broccoli and continue boiling for 4 minutes. Add peas and continue boiling for 3 additional minutes. Drain.

3. Heat oil in a medium saucepot over medium heat. Add entire can of tomatoes with liquid, breaking up tomatoes with your hands. Add oregano, basil, and black pepper. Bring to a boil over high heat, then lower heat and simmer uncovered for 30 minutes.

4. Add broccoli and peas to the pot with the tomatoes and continue cooking for an additional 3 minutes until vegetables are heated through. Stir pasta into pot until covered with sauce, then serve.

PER SERVING | Calories: 345 | Fat: 5g | Protein: 13g | Sodium: 300mg | Fiber: 8g | Carbohydrates: 64g | Sugar: 9g

Pasta il Tricolore

This dish gets its name from the Italian flag—sporting a green, red, and white color scheme. For a fast workday dinner, prep the ingredients ahead. Then, all that's needed is a quick toss-up before serving.

INGREDIENTS | SERVES 4

12 ounces gluten-free pasta

2 small red potatoes, cut into 1" cubes

1 cup chopped green beans

1 teaspoon grapeseed oil

¼ teaspoon sea salt

⅛ teaspoon freshly ground black pepper

⅓ cup Sun-Dried Tomato Pesto (see recipe in Chapter 9)

1 teaspoon walnut oil

Tips for Cooking Gluten-Free Pasta

Gluten-free pasta runs the risk of either sticking together or getting too soggy. Be sure to cook the pasta in a pot large enough so that the pasta is not over-crowded. Don't add any oil to the pot and be sure to stir the pasta frequently. Taste the pasta periodically to ensure that it is cooked just right.

1. Cook pasta according to package directions.

2. Preheat oven to 400°F. Line a baking sheet with parchment paper. Scatter potatoes and beans on sheet; toss with grapeseed oil, salt, and pepper. Roast 20–30 minutes, tossing halfway through.

3. In a large bowl, toss cooked pasta with pesto. Add roasted vegetables and toss again.

4. Drizzle with walnut oil. If a thinner pesto consistency is desired, toss again. Serve immediately.

PER SERVING | Calories: 560 | Fat: 17g | Protein: 18g | Sodium: 495mg | Fiber: 6g | Carbohydrates: 85g | Sugar: 6g

Macaroni and Cheese

This recipe features a blend of creamy low-FODMAP cheeses and a sprinkle of garden-fresh chives—resulting in an elegant version of a kid-friendly classic.

INGREDIENTS | SERVES 6

12 ounces gluten-free elbow macaroni

2 slices gluten-free bread, toasted

½ cup Parmesan cheese

2 tablespoons extra-virgin olive oil, divided

2 teaspoons sea salt, divided

½ teaspoon freshly ground pepper, divided

2 tablespoons melted butter, divided

¼ cup gluten-free sweet rice flour

2 cups lactose-free milk

1½ cups cubed Brie cheese, rind removed

1½ cups cubed Camembert cheese, rind removed

½ cup chopped fresh chives

1. Cook pasta according to package directions, to an al dente texture.

2. Add toast, Parmesan, 1 tablespoon oil, 1 teaspoon salt, ¼ teaspoon pepper, and 1 tablespoon butter to a food processor. Pulse to form bread crumbs.

3. Preheat oven to 375°F. In a large stockpot over medium-low heat, add remaining butter and oil. When bubbling, add flour and whisk constantly for 1–2 minutes until thickened and light golden brown.

4. Whisk in milk, ¼ cup at a time, until thickened and bubbling—about 8–10 minutes. Season with remaining salt and pepper.

5. Fold in Brie and Camembert until fully melted. Add the cooked macaroni and stir to combine.

6. Pour into a 13" × 9" baking dish or 6 one-cup ovenproof ramekins. Sprinkle bread crumb mixture evenly over the top.

7. Bake 25–30 minutes, until sauce begins to bubble and top is evenly browned. Top with chopped fresh chives and serve.

PER SERVING | Calories: 520 | Fat: 39g | Protein: 27g | Sodium: 1,750mg | Fiber: 0g | Carbohydrates: 16g | Sugar: 5g

Creamy Chicken Lasagna

Great for entertaining, this rich, impressive main dish can be assembled
a day ahead and put into the oven when guests arrive.

INGREDIENTS | SERVES 8

9 gluten-free lasagna noodles
1 tablespoon extra-virgin olive oil
10 ounces baby spinach leaves
¼ teaspoon sea salt
2 cups Roasted Tomato Sauce (see recipe in Chapter 9)
1½ cups Alfredo Sauce (see recipe in Chapter 9)
1½ cups chopped grilled chicken
¾ cup freshly grated Parmesan cheese
½ cup grated mozzarella cheese

1. Cook pasta according to package directions, to an al dente texture.

2. Heat oil in a medium skillet over medium-low heat.

3. Add spinach and salt, sauté until wilted, stirring frequently. Set aside to cool.

4. Mix cooled spinach with Roasted Tomato Sauce.

5. Preheat oven to 350°F. Spread ⅓ cup of Alfredo Sauce on bottom of a 13" × 9" baking dish. Top with 3 lasagna noodles, side by side to fill dish. Spread another layer of Alfredo sauce on top of noodles. Sprinkle ½ cup chopped chicken over sauce.

6. Spoon 1 cup of spinach-tomato mixture on top. Sprinkle with ¼ cup Parmesan.

7. Repeat, creating another noodle, Alfredo sauce, chicken, spinach-tomato mixture, Parmesan layer. Cover with 3 remaining lasagna noodles.

8. Mix remaining ½ cup of Alfredo sauce and chicken. Spread over noodles, sprinkle with mozzarella and remaining Parmesan cheese.

9. Bake 30 minutes until cheese is melted. Let sit for 5 minutes, then serve.

PER SERVING | Calories: 355 | Fat: 20g | Protein: 24g | Sodium: 1,150mg | Fiber: 2g | Carbohydrates: 20g | Sugar: 5g

Penne alla Vodka

The vodka adds a signature touch to this Italian classic—but feel free to omit it for alcohol-free fare that's equally delish.

4 cups cooked gluten-free penne

2 tablespoons butter

1 medium sweet yellow onion, peeled and quartered

1½ cups diced tomatoes

1 teaspoon turbinado sugar

1 teaspoon sea salt

¼ teaspoon crushed red pepper

1½ cups Tomato Purée (see recipe in Chapter 9)

⅓ cup vodka

1 cup frozen sweet peas, thawed

2 tablespoons Whipped Cream (see recipe in Chapter 14)

½ cup freshly grated Parmesan cheese

1. Cook pasta according to package directions.

2. Heat butter in a large saucepan over medium-low heat. Add onion; sauté until fragrant. Remove and discard onion.

3. To butter, add tomatoes, sugar, salt, and pepper. Sauté 10 minutes, stirring occasionally.

4. Add purée and vodka. Bring just to a boil, then lower heat and simmer uncovered 30 minutes. Stir in peas.

5. Fold in whipped cream until combined. Divide pasta, topped with sauce, evenly among 4 plates. Sprinkle Parmesan on top and serve.

PER SERVING | Calories: 500 | Fat: 16g | Protein: 17g | Sodium: 1,415mg | Fiber: 8g | Carbohydrates: 61g | Sugar: 11g

Lasagna Pepperonata

Here's a rich, elegant take on a traditional lasagna preparation. Omit the beef and this recipe makes a lovely vegetarian main dish.

INGREDIENTS | SERVES 8

9 gluten-free lasagna noodles

1 pound lean ground beef

1 teaspoon dried oregano

1 teaspoon dried basil

⅛ teaspoon sea salt

⅛ teaspoon freshly ground black pepper

⅛ teaspoon ground nutmeg

6 cups Pepperonata Sauce (see recipe in Chapter 9), divided

8 ounces Brie, trimmed, thinly sliced, divided

¾ cup freshly grated Parmesan cheese, divided

½ cup grated mozzarella cheese

1. Cook lasagna according to package directions, to an al dente texture.

2. Heat oven to 350°F. In a medium skillet over medium heat, brown beef. Drain and season with oregano, basil, salt, pepper, and nutmeg.

3. Purée 3 cups Pepperonata Sauce in a food processor.

4. Spread ¾ cup of puréed sauce on bottom of a 13" × 9" baking dish. Top with 3 lasagna noodles side by side to fill dish.

5. Spread another ¾ cup of puréed sauce over noodles. Scatter a third of the Brie slices on top.

6. Sprinkle 1 cup ground beef over Brie and noodles. Top with 1½ cups non-puréed sauce and ¼ cup Parmesan.

7. Repeat with another layer, starting with noodles and then puréed sauce, Brie, beef, non-puréed sauce, and Parmesan. Cover with remaining 3 lasagna noodles.

8. In a small bowl, mix any remaining beef with remaining puréed sauce. Spread on top of noodles. Sprinkle Parmesan and mozzarella cheeses evenly on top.

9. Bake for 30 minutes until cheese is melted. Let sit for 5 minutes, then serve.

PER SERVING | Calories: 355 | Fat: 18g | Protein: 26g | Sodium: 505mg | Fiber: 4g | Carbohydrates: 21g | Sugar: 7g

Colorful Penne Toss

Prep the ingredients ahead, then toss just before serving, for a quick midweek supper.

INGREDIENTS | SERVES 8

1 pound gluten-free penne

2 tablespoons extra-virgin olive oil

1 teaspoon balsamic vinegar

⅛ teaspoon sea salt

¼ teaspoon freshly ground black pepper

8 ounces mozzarella cheese, cut into 1" cubes

¼ cup freshly grated Parmesan cheese, divided

2 cups packed baby spinach leaves

4 gluten-, onion-, garlic-free sausage links, cooked, cut into ½" slices

1 cup sliced grape tomatoes

2 tablespoons pitted, diced olives

2 tablespoons fresh basil leaves, torn

1. Cook pasta according to package directions.

2. While pasta is cooking, make dressing: Whisk olive oil, vinegar, salt, and pepper in a small bowl.

3. In a large pasta bowl, toss mozzarella cubes with 2 tablespoons of Parmesan. Add spinach, sausage, tomatoes, and olives, and toss again.

4. When pasta is cooked, drain completely and, while still piping hot, add to pasta bowl with dressing. Toss to combine.

5. Sprinkle with remaining Parmesan cheese, fresh basil, and serve.

PER SERVING | Calories: 385 | Fat: 15g | Protein: 17g | Sodium: 385mg | Fiber: 2g | Carbohydrates: 44g | Sugar: 2g

Sausages and the Low-FODMAP Diet

You must be very selective with the sausages that you choose to eat. Many sausages contain gluten, onion, and/or garlic, all of which would make them unsuitable for the diet. Ideally, you could consult with a local butcher shop to find out exactly what ingredients are used in its products.

Skillet Swirls

This one-pot wonder is as pretty as it is delicious. The ingredients can be prepared a day or two ahead, saving you time on assembly day.

INGREDIENTS | SERVES 8

¾ pound ground beef, cooked and cooled

1½ cups Alfredo Sauce (see recipe in Chapter 9)

4 cups Traditional Tomato Sauce (see recipe in Chapter 9), divided

12 gluten-free lasagna noodles, cooked and cooled

½ cup shredded mozzarella cheese

¼ cup shredded Parmesan cheese

1. In a medium bowl, combine cooked beef with Alfredo Sauce.

2. Spread 2 cups of Traditional Tomato Sauce on bottom of a large ovenproof skillet.

3. Preheat oven to 375°F. Lay lasagna noodles flat on a nonstick workspace. Spread a thin layer of creamy beef mixture on each noodle, avoiding the edges. Then roll it up, jelly-roll style, and place it seam-side down in the skillet. Repeat until all noodles are rolled up and in skillet.

4. Pour remaining tomato sauce evenly over the tops of the rolls, filling in any gaps.

5. Sprinkle with mozzarella and Parmesan cheese and bake for 20–25 minutes or until cheese on top is melted and sauce is bubbling. Let sit for 5 minutes, then serve.

PER SERVING | Calories: 418 | Fat: 25g | Protein: 22g | Sodium: 1,060mg | Fiber: 3g | Carbohydrates: 28g | Sugar: 9g

Garden Pasta

This mega-healthy dish calls for veggie pasta—made from long, thin shards of carrots and zucchini. You can trim the pasta by hand, or use a spiralizing tool for quicker results.

INGREDIENTS | SERVES 4

1 large zucchini, spiralized

4 large carrots, peeled and spiralized

1 tablespoon extra-virgin olive oil

2 cups Roasted Tomato Sauce (see recipe in Chapter 9)

8 Kalamata olives, pitted

4 pieces sun-dried tomatoes, chopped

½ cup Parmesan cheese

1. In a large bowl, toss the vegetables with the oil.

2. Add Roasted Tomato Sauce, olives, and sun-dried tomatoes, and toss again.

3. Sprinkle with Parmesan and serve.

PER SERVING | Calories: 250 | Fat: 14g | Protein: 8g | Sodium: 910mg | Fiber: 5g | Carbohydrates: 25g | Sugar: 10g

Spiralizers

A spiralizer might be a nice thing to treat yourself to as a reward for being disciplined with your diet. A spiralizer is a hand-cranked appliance that carves vegetables into long, thin, pasta-like shapes. Since you will be avoiding gluten, vegetable pasta makes for a nice alternative.

Beef, Pork, and Poultry

Autumn's Roast Chicken

Once in the oven, this simple roast chicken with autumnal rub will cast a fragrant spell over your kitchen. After carving, be sure to drizzle each serving with Autumn's Glaze (see recipe in Chapter 9). The carcass makes a great base for Basic Roast Chicken Stock (see recipe in Chapter 8).

INGREDIENTS | SERVES 4

1½ tablespoons butter
1 tablespoon canned pumpkin
1 tablespoon pure maple syrup
1 teaspoon ground cinnamon
1 teaspoon dried thyme
½ teaspoon sea salt
¼ teaspoon freshly ground black pepper
1 (4-pound) whole chicken

Canned Pumpkin

You need to be cautious when purchasing canned pumpkin, because there is a very similar-looking canned product known as pumpkin pie filling. Pumpkin pie filling contains ingredients that may not be appropriate for a low-FODMAP diet. Pure canned pumpkin should be nothing but pumpkin and so can be enjoyed for its nutrition without worry.

1. Preheat oven to 375°F.

2. Melt butter in a small saucepan. Stir in pumpkin, maple syrup, cinnamon, and thyme. Season with salt and pepper. Refrigerate for 10 minutes.

3. Cut small slit under skin on both sides of chicken breast and under legs. Once the pumpkin mixture is cool, generously rub it under skin and all over the top of skin. Place chicken, breast side up, on the rack of a roasting pan. Roast 50–60 minutes, or until a meat thermometer registers 165°F at thickest part of thigh.

4. Tent with foil for 5 minutes before carving.

PER SERVING | Calories: 543 | Fat: 12g | Protein: 98g | Sodium: 525mg | Fiber: 1g | Carbohydrates: 4g | Sugar: 3g

Chinese Chicken

If you find yourself craving Chinese food, this dish hits the spot—
with traditional flavorings, plenty of veggies, and rice.

INGREDIENTS | SERVES 4

¾ cup arrowroot powder

½ cup white wine, divided

½ cup gluten-free tamari, divided

1 pound boneless, skinless chicken breasts, cubed

½ teaspoon sugar

½ cup Basic Roast Chicken Stock (see recipe in Chapter 8)

2 tablespoons sesame oil, divided

1 teaspoon natural peanut butter

4 garlic cloves, peeled and slightly smashed

1 cup broccoli florets

1 cup sliced red bell pepper

2 cups cooked brown rice

1. In a medium bowl, stir to combine arrowroot and ¼ cup each of wine and tamari. Add chicken; stir to coat. Cover and refrigerate for 30 minutes.

2. Transfer chicken to a colander and drain marinade completely. Set chicken aside.

3. In a separate bowl, combine sugar, stock, and remaining wine and tamari.

4. In another small bowl, whisk 1 tablespoon oil and peanut butter.

5. Heat remaining oil over medium-high heat in a large wok or skillet. Add the garlic and sauté, stirring constantly, until softened and brown at the edges, about 2 minutes. Remove garlic from pan and discard, leaving oil.

6. Add chicken and stir-fry quickly, browning chicken on all sides—approximately 8–10 minutes. (Lower heat if chicken is browning too quickly.) Scrape up and discard any loose marinade bits. Once fully cooked through, transfer chicken to a plate and cover to keep warm.

7. Add broccoli and bell pepper to skillet and quickly stir-fry for 1 minute. Add stock and peanut butter mixtures and stir. Cover, then lower heat and simmer for 5–8 minutes, until vegetables are crisp-tender.

8. Divide rice, chicken, and vegetables in their sauce evenly among four plates and serve.

PER SERVING | Calories: 458 | Fat: 11g | Protein: 30g | Sodium: 2,014mg | Fiber: 4g | Carbohydrates: 53g | Sugar: 3.5g

Caramel Oat Chicken Fingers

This is a great dish to make with and serve to the kids.

INGREDIENTS | SERVES 4

1 teaspoon butter

1 cup gluten-free rolled oats

¼ teaspoon sea salt

1 teaspoon maple sugar

2 large eggs

1 teaspoon ground cinnamon

4 (3-ounce) boneless, skinless chicken breasts, pounded and cut into 1"-wide strips

1. Heat oven to 400°F. Line a baking sheet with parchment paper and coat with coconut oil spray.

2. In a medium skillet, melt butter over medium heat. Add oats and stir. Add salt and maple sugar and stir to combine. Lower heat and stir until oats start to toast and turn light brown. Transfer oat mixture to plate to cool.

3. While oat mixture is cooling, whisk eggs in a bowl. Add cinnamon to cooled oat mixture and stir to combine.

4. Dip chicken strips in egg and then in oat mixture to fully coat all sides.

5. Place strips on baking sheet and bake for 15–20 minutes or until chicken is fully cooked. Transfer to a platter and serve.

PER SERVING | Calories: 220 | Fat: 7g | Protein: 24g | Sodium: 281mg | Fiber: 2g | Carbohydrates: 15g | Sugar: 2g

Maple Mustard Barbecued Chicken

This recipe can serve as an easy weeknight dinner or be the main course at your next summer barbecue. No one needs to know it's low in FODMAPs!

8 bone-in, skinless chicken thighs

½ cup brown mustard

1 tablespoon brown sugar

2 tablespoons pure maple syrup

1 tablespoon white wine vinegar

1 tablespoon gluten-free tamari

¼ teaspoon sea salt

¼ teaspoon freshly ground black pepper

Rosemary Red Potatoes

Serve these crunchy potatoes alongside your barbecued chicken thighs. Simply quarter 6 small red potatoes and toss with a tablespoon of olive oil and a tablespoon of rosemary. Roast in a 400°F oven for 30 minutes, stirring after 15 minutes. Season with salt and pepper just before serving.

1. Fill a large stockpot with water and bring to a boil over high heat. Add chicken. When water has returned to a boil, set a timer and continue boiling for 20 minutes.

2. Combine all other ingredients in a medium bowl. Remove and reserve ¼ cup of the resulting sauce.

3. After chicken has finished parboiling, allow it to cool (about 15 minutes), then place in a large bowl. Cover with remaining barbecue sauce and marinate in the refrigerator for at least 30 minutes.

4. Preheat broiler for five minutes while placing chicken on an oiled grill rack. Place chicken under broiler and cook, 6–8 minutes per side. Serve with reserved sauce.

PER SERVING | Calories: 228 | Fat: 7g | Protein: 29g | Sodium: 848mg | Fiber: 1g | Carbohydrates: 12g | Sugar: 10g

Smoky Sourdough Pizza

Yes, you can enjoy pizza on a low-FODMAP diet! This recipe uses the crust from a loaf of sourdough bread as the base. You can use the leftover sourdough bread from this recipe for the Savory Sourdough Strata in Chapter 6.

INGREDIENTS | SERVES 4

2 tablespoons extra-virgin olive oil

2 garlic cloves, peeled, slightly smashed

8 pieces smoked sun-dried tomatoes, diced, divided

8 ounces smoked Brie, trimmed, cut to 1" cubes

6 ounces smoked ham, cut to ½" cubes

1 cup seeded, diced tomatoes

¼ cup pitted, diced Kalamata olives

⅛ teaspoon sea salt

⅛ teaspoon freshly ground black pepper

1 gluten-free sourdough loaf, insides removed

½ cup freshly grated Parmesan cheese

½ cup thinly sliced kale leaves, stems removed

1. Heat oven to 400°F. Line a baking sheet with parchment paper.

2. Heat oil in a small skillet over medium heat. Add garlic and half of the sun-dried tomatoes and stir until fragrant, about 1 minute. Remove from heat and set aside to cool. Once cool, remove and discard garlic.

3. Transfer oil with tomatoes to a medium bowl. Toss in remaining sun-dried tomatoes, Brie, ham, diced tomatoes, and olives. Season with salt and pepper and toss again.

4. Cut bread crust into 4 even pieces and place on baking sheet. Fill each piece with an even amount of the tomato/ham/Brie mixture, spreading in an even layer. Top with Parmesan cheese and kale.

5. Bake 5–8 minutes or until crusts turn light brown and cheese melts.

PER SERVING | Calories: 352 | Fat: 26g | Protein: 22g | Sodium: 807mg | Fiber: 1g | Carbohydrates: 7.5g | Sugar: 3g

Turkey Cutlets with Grapes

This elegant supper can be customized for all seasons: Use green grapes in spring and summer and a mixture of reds in fall and winter.

INGREDIENTS | SERVES 4

2 cups seedless grapes, divided
¼ cup coconut milk
¼ teaspoon freshly grated ginger
⅛ teaspoon pure vanilla extract
⅛ teaspoon sea salt
⅛ teaspoon freshly ground black pepper
1 cup Basic Roast Chicken Stock (see recipe in Chapter 8)
½ cup oat flour
¼ cup shredded unsweetened coconut
1 pound boneless turkey cutlets, pounded to ½" thickness

Cooking Seasonally

There is something extra-nice about varying your cooking according to the season. In addition to getting your vegetables and fruits at their freshest, grown in their most natural state, eating seasonally helps you to be mindful of your connection to the world—a state of mind that will enhance your overall health.

1. Slice 1 cup of whole grapes into halves and set aside.

2. Add second cup of grapes to a small pot of boiling water and blanch for 1 minute. Drain and cool. When cool enough to handle, peel skins off grapes.

3. Add skinless grapes, coconut milk, ginger, vanilla, salt, and pepper to a blender and process until smooth.

4. In a small saucepan over medium heat, bring stock to a boil. Lower heat and simmer uncovered 15 minutes. Whisk in puréed grape mixture and simmer uncovered 15 minutes more.

5. In a flat dish, mix flour and coconut. Dredge each cutlet in flour mixture.

6. Heat a large skillet coated with coconut oil spray over medium-high heat. Add floured cutlets and cook, 5–8 minutes per side, until lightly browned on all sides and fully cooked through. Transfer to a serving platter.

7. Add sliced grapes to sauce in pan and heat for 2 minutes. Pour sauce over cutlets and serve.

PER SERVING | Calories: 268 | Fat: 14g | Protein: 20.5g | Sodium: 321mg | Fiber: 1g | Carbohydrates: 16g | Sugar: 12.5g

Barbecue Pork Macaroni and Cheese

This sweet and savory blend of flavors is a real crowd pleaser. Remove the meats and substitute low-FODMAP vegetable stock for the chicken stock and this recipe makes a wonderful vegetarian main dish.

INGREDIENTS | SERVES 8

1 (1-pound) box gluten-free macaroni

1½ cups peeled and cubed butternut squash

1 teaspoon extra-virgin olive oil

1 teaspoon sea salt, divided

½ teaspoon freshly ground black pepper, divided

¼ teaspoon nutmeg

¼ teaspoon ground ginger

½ pound boneless pork loin, cut into ½" cubes

¼ cup Sweet Barbecue Sauce (see recipe in Chapter 9)

¾ cup Basic Roast Chicken Stock (see recipe in Chapter 8)

¾ cup coconut milk

1½ cups shredded Cheddar cheese, divided

1 cup loosely packed, thinly sliced kale leaves

2 slices bacon, cooked, cooled, and crumbled

½ cup freshly grated Parmesan cheese

1. Cook macaroni according to package directions, to an al dente texture. Drain and pour macaroni into a 13" × 9" baking dish. Set aside.

2. Heat oven to 375°F. On a parchment-lined baking sheet, toss squash with olive oil. Sprinkle with ½ teaspoon salt, ¼ teaspoon pepper, nutmeg, and ginger. Bake for 25 minutes. Remove from oven and set aside to cool.

3. In a medium skillet over medium heat, brown all sides of pork. Add barbecue sauce; toss to coat. Simmer uncovered for 1–2 minutes, remove from heat, and set aside to cool.

4. Transfer squash to the bowl of a food processor. Add stock, milk, and remaining salt and pepper and process to combine. Add 1 cup Cheddar cheese and pulse until combined.

5. Pour squash mixture over macaroni and stir to combine.

6. Tuck kale here and there, between the noodles. Dot top of casserole evenly with the barbecue pork cubes and bacon.

7. Sprinkle top of casserole evenly with remaining ½ cup Cheddar and Parmesan. Bake 20 minutes, or until cheese is melted and bubbling or browning. Let sit for 5 minutes, then serve.

PER SERVING | Calories: 452 | Fat: 18g | Protein: 21.5g | Sodium: 693mg | Fiber: 2.5g | Carbohydrates: 50g | Sugar: 4g

Italian Chicken with Vegetables

This recipe is so good that even the pickiest of eaters will be happily eating their vegetables. The use of almond flour, at a FODMAP-friendly level, gives the sauce a nice texture and a sweet taste.

INGREDIENTS | SERVES 4

1 (1-pound) package gluten-free spaghetti

4 (3-ounce) boneless, skinless chicken breasts

½ cup almond flour

2 tablespoons extra-virgin olive oil

1 medium green bell pepper, seeded and diced

1 medium red bell pepper, seeded and diced

1 medium zucchini, sliced lengthwise and cut into ¼" slices

2 cups Traditional Tomato Sauce (see recipe in Chapter 9)

4 ounces mozzarella, thinly sliced

1. Cook pasta according to package directions. Drain and set aside.

2. Slice the chicken breast into thin cutlets. Place the almond flour in a shallow dish and dredge chicken until coated on both sides.

3. In a large skillet, heat olive oil over medium-high heat. Add chicken and brown on both sides, approximately 2 minutes per side. Remove chicken from pan and place in a shallow dish.

4. Reduce heat to medium and add bell peppers and zucchini to oil and drippings. Sauté vegetables for approximately 8 minutes, until tender but still crispy.

5. Return chicken to the pan, placing the cutlets on top of vegetables. Pour in tomato sauce and raise heat to high. Bring sauce to a boil, then lower heat and simmer, covered, for 15 minutes. Check to make sure that chicken is cooked through.

6. Place the mozzarella slices on the chicken. Continue to simmer, covered, for another 4 minutes until cheese has melted.

7. Serve chicken and vegetables over the spaghetti.

PER SERVING | Calories: 788 | Fat: 24g | Protein: 44g | Sodium: 928mg | Fiber: 8.5g | Carbohydrates: 99g | Sugar: 12g

Grilled Chicken Parmigiana

Here is an easy, healthy take on an Italian classic. Serve with some gluten-free spaghetti and a FODMAP-friendly vegetable side, such as Garlic-Infused Spinach (see recipe in Chapter 13), for a complete dinner.

INGREDIENTS | SERVES 4

1 pound skinless, boneless chicken breast, cut into thin cutlets

½ cup Traditional Tomato Sauce (see recipe in Chapter 9)

16 fresh basil leaves, sliced into thin strips

8 ounces mozzarella cheese, thinly sliced

1. Heat a charcoal or gas grill to 350°F. Cook chicken 3 minutes per side or until cooked through.

2. With chicken still on grill, place 1 tablespoon of sauce and a small pile of basil on top of each cutlet. Cover with 2 mozzarella slices. Continue to grill until cheese has melted, approximately 3 minutes. Serve.

PER SERVING | Calories: 303 | Fat: 15g | Protein: 37g | Sodium: 642mg | Fiber: 0.5g | Carbohydrates: 3g | Sugar: 2g

Southampton Chili

This could also be known as "Meat Lover's Chili," as the high-FODMAP beans are swapped out for gluten-free sausage. You can serve it over some brown rice for a more filling meal.

INGREDIENTS | SERVES 8

1 pound lean ground beef

1 (7-ounce) package garlic-, onion- and gluten-free breakfast sausage

1 (28-ounce) can whole tomatoes, broken up slightly

1 red pepper, seeded and diced

1 medium green bell pepper, seeded and diced

1 bay leaf

2 tablespoons ground cumin

2 tablespoons ground oregano

⅛ teaspoon ground red pepper

1. Over medium heat, brown ground beef in a large stockpot until cooked through. Drain off excess fat and return to stockpot on the stove.

2. In a small skillet, brown sausage according to package directions. Slice each sausage in half lengthwise, then cut into ¼" half-rounds.

3. Place all ingredients, including sausage, into the stockpot with the beef. Bring to a boil over high heat, then lower heat and simmer, uncovered, for 2 hours. Discard bay leaf and serve.

PER SERVING | Calories: 145 | Fat: 3g | Protein: 5g | Sodium: 185mg | Fiber: 2g | Carbohydrates: 14g | Sugar: 3g

Garden Veggie Dip Burgers

This is a nice way to sneak some vegetables onto your dinner plate. Be sure to allow time to refrigerate burgers for at least 12 hours before grilling.

INGREDIENTS | SERVES 4

2 tablespoons light sour cream

1 large carrot, peeled and diced

½ medium red bell pepper, seeded and diced

½ cup packed baby spinach leaves, chopped

1 teaspoon sea salt

1 pound lean ground beef

Sour Cream and the Low-FODMAP Diet

Sour cream comes from cow's milk and therefore contains some lactose, which is restricted in the low-FODMAP diet. However, light sour cream has less lactose and therefore small amounts (no more than 2 tablespoons) can be tolerated. This means that you can still enjoy the creaminess that sour cream can add to a recipe.

1. In a food processor, blend sour cream, carrot, pepper, spinach, and salt until creamy.

2. In a large bowl, add vegetable mixture to ground beef and mix to combine. Make 4 patties. Refrigerate patties for 12–24 hours before grilling.

3. Heat a charcoal or gas grill to 350°F. Cook patties on grill to an internal temperature of 160°F, about 5 minutes per side.

PER SERVING | Calories: 177 | Fat: 7g | Protein: 25g | Sodium: 680mg | Fiber: 1g | Carbohydrates: 3g | Sugar: 2g

Sourdough Meatballs

You can still enjoy meatballs on the low-FODMAP diet if you don't use gluten-containing bread crumbs. The toasted sourdough bread crumbs add a zest to these classic savory meatballs.

INGREDIENTS | SERVES 4

1 slice gluten-free sourdough bread, toasted

1 large egg

¼ cup freshly grated Parmesan cheese

1 teaspoon sea salt

½ teaspoon freshly ground black pepper

½ pound meatloaf mix (beef, pork, and veal)

1. Pulse bread in a food processor to create coarse crumbs.

2. In a large bowl, whisk egg, cheese, salt, and pepper. Add bread crumbs and meat. Hand-mix just until combined.

3. Preheat broiler. Form mixture into 16 equally sized balls and place on a foil-lined baking sheet. Broil for 8–10 minutes, or until tops are evenly browned. Remove sheet, carefully turn meatballs over, and broil for 8–10 minutes more, or until fully cooked. Serve.

PER SERVING | Calories: 168 | Fat: 9g | Protein: 16g | Sodium: 805mg | Fiber: 0g | Carbohydrates: 5g | Sugar: 0g

CHAPTER 12

Fish and Shellfish

Shrimp with Cherry Tomatoes

The cherry tomatoes give a pop of flavor to this colorful dish. The vegetables are so spaghetti-like, you could skip the pasta altogether. Feel free to use a spiralizer for the zucchini and carrot prep.

INGREDIENTS | SERVES 4

1 pound gluten-free spaghetti

2 medium zucchini, trimmed

1 pound carrots, peeled

3 tablespoons extra-virgin olive oil, divided

1 pint cherry tomatoes, halved

3 tablespoons butter

3 tablespoons white wine

Juice of 1 medium lemon

2 tablespoons chopped fresh basil

2 cloves garlic, peeled and slightly crushed

1½ pounds peeled and deveined shrimp

⅛ teaspoon sea salt

⅛ teaspoon freshly ground black pepper

1. Cook spaghetti according to package directions.

2. With vegetable peeler, peel zucchini and carrots into long strips. Heat 1 tablespoon of oil in a large skillet over medium heat. Add vegetables and sauté until soft, approximately 5–8 minutes, stirring frequently. Transfer to a bowl and keep warm. Wipe the skillet clean with a paper towel.

3. In a medium skillet, combine tomatoes, butter, wine, lemon juice, and basil. Cook over low heat for 10 minutes, stirring occasionally, then keep warm.

4. While tomatoes are cooking, heat the remaining 2 tablespoons of oil in the large skillet over medium heat. Add garlic and sauté until just starting to brown, about 5 minutes. Remove garlic and add shrimp to oil. Sauté shrimp until cooked through, approximately 8 minutes, stirring frequently. Season with salt and pepper.

5. To serve, place spaghetti on a serving platter and top with vegetable mixture, shrimp, and tomato mixture.

PER SERVING | Calories: 848 | Fat: 24g | Protein: 52g | Sodium: 420mg | Fiber: 9g | Carbohydrates: 103g | Sugar: 13g

Glazed Salmon

With this salmon on your plate, you will experience the perfect blend of sweet and savory. This dish pairs wonderfully with Garlicky Smashed Potatoes (see recipe in Chapter 13).

INGREDIENTS | SERVES 4

¼ cup gluten-free tamari
1 tablespoon almond butter
1 tablespoon pure maple syrup
2 teaspoons rice vinegar
2 teaspoons sesame oil
1 teaspoon blackstrap molasses
⅛ teaspoon ground ginger
12-ounce fillet of salmon

Salmon for Health

Salmon is a great source of omega-3 fatty acids. These "healthy fats" reduce inflammation in our bodies, protect us from heart disease, and appear to play a role in brain health. Whenever possible, purchase wild salmon over farmed salmon, as the wild-caught salmon contains a higher amount of omega-3s.

1. Make glaze: Mix all ingredients except salmon in a small saucepan.

2. Transfer 2 tablespoons glaze to a small bowl.

3. Heat a charcoal grill, gas grill, or broiler to 350°F. Grill or broil salmon, skin-side down, for 15 minutes, basting with the sauce in the small bowl.

4. While salmon is cooking, heat remaining glaze over medium-low heat for about 5 minutes to thicken.

5. When salmon is fully cooked, remove from heat, drizzle with heated glaze, and serve.

PER SERVING | Calories: 190 | Fat: 10g | Protein: 19g | Sodium: 955mg | Fiber: 0g | Carbohydrates: 6g | Sugar: 4g

Grilled Cod with Fresh Basil

Although this dish can be prepared all year long, the combination of fresh basil and freshly squeezed lemon makes for a "plate full of summer."

INGREDIENTS | SERVES 4

3 tablespoons extra-virgin olive oil

Juice of 1 medium lemon

2 pounds cod fillet

1 garlic clove, peeled, slightly smashed

8 tablespoons butter (1 stick)

2 tablespoons chopped fresh basil

1 pinch ground red pepper

1. Combine oil and lemon juice in a shallow dish. Add cod and turn to coat. Marinate for 30 minutes at room temperature.

2. Heat a charcoal or gas grill to 350°F. Grill fish for 15 minutes or until cooked through, flipping once after 8 minutes.

3. When fish is on its second side, put garlic and butter in a small saucepan and cook over low heat for 5 minutes. Turn off heat, remove and discard the garlic, and add basil and ground red pepper.

4. Remove cod from grill and serve with basil sauce on the side.

PER SERVING | Calories: 400 | Fat: 25g | Protein: 40g | Sodium: 125mg | Fiber: 0g | Carbohydrates: 1g | Sugar: 0g

Salmon Noodle Casserole

Just because you are following a low-FODMAP diet does not mean you cannot enjoy comfort foods—you just need to be a little creative. Enjoy this sweeter, more nutritious spin on the classic tuna noodle casserole.

INGREDIENTS | SERVES 8

3 small sweet potatoes

1 pound gluten-free egg noodles

¼ cup Sweet Barbecue Sauce (see recipe in Chapter 9)

1 (5-ounce) can salmon, drained and flaked with a fork

1 cup freshly grated Parmesan cheese, divided

2 slices gluten-free bread, toasted

½ cup shelled pecans

1 teaspoon sea salt, divided

½ teaspoon freshly ground pepper, divided

¾ cup lactose-free whole milk

¼ cup lactose-free plain low-fat yogurt

1 cup Vegetable Stock (see recipe in Chapter 8)

1 cup shredded fontina cheese

1 cup packed baby spinach leaves

1. Preheat oven to 400°F. Poke a few holes in each sweet potato and place in a small baking dish. Bake sweet potatoes for 45 minutes. Remove from oven, slice open to cool, and set aside.

2. Cook noodles according to package directions to an al dente texture.

3. Heat barbecue sauce in a small skillet over medium heat. Add salmon and sauté very carefully for about 3 minutes until fully coated. Remove from heat.

4. In a food processor, add ½ cup Parmesan cheese, toast, pecans, ½ teaspoon salt, and ¼ teaspoon pepper. Pulse to a bread-crumb consistency. Transfer to a medium bowl.

5. Once cool enough to handle, scoop inside flesh from sweet potatoes and transfer to food processor. Add milk, yogurt, stock, and remaining salt and pepper and process to combine.

6. Add fontina and remaining ½ cup Parmesan cheese and pulse until combined.

7. Transfer noodles to a 13" × 9" baking dish. Pour sweet potato mixture over noodles and stir to combine.

8. Tuck spinach leaves between the noodles. Dot top of casserole evenly with salmon mixture.

9. Sprinkle top of casserole evenly with bread-crumb mixture. Bake 20 minutes, or until cheese is melted and bubbling or browning. Let sit for 5 minutes, then serve.

PER SERVING | Calories: 510 | Fat: 19g | Protein: 25g | Sodium: 1,140mg | Fiber: 5g | Carbohydrates: 61g | Sugar: 8g

Fish and Chips

This recipe favors good health by baking the fish and potatoes, rather than frying them—but the millet coating adds the familiar crunch of fried fish.

INGREDIENTS | SERVES 4

¼ cup millet
¼ cup chopped pecans
2 tablespoons cornmeal
1½ teaspoons sea salt, divided
⅛ teaspoon ground red pepper
4 small red potatoes, thinly sliced
1 tablespoon extra-virgin olive oil
½ cup lactose-free 2% milk
2 tablespoons light sour cream
12 ounces tilapia fillets

Corn and the Low-FODMAP Diet

On the low-FODMAP diet, sweet corn is limited to a half of a cob, as eating the whole cob would expose you to high levels of GOS and sorbitol. However, products such as cornmeal, cornstarch, and popcorn are permitted because they are made from a different variety of corn.

1. In a medium bowl, cover millet with boiling water and soak for 30 minutes.

2. Preheat oven to 400°F. Line 2 baking sheets with parchment paper.

3. Drain millet completely and spread on one baking sheet. Add pecans to second baking sheet. Roast millet and pecans for 10 minutes, tossing halfway through.

4. Process pecans in a food processor until finely ground. Transfer to a medium shallow dish; toss with millet, cornmeal, ½ teaspoon salt, and red pepper.

5. Toss potato slices in oil and 1 teaspoon salt. Re-line one baking sheet and scatter it with potatoes. Roast in oven for 30 minutes or until brown and crisp.

6. In another shallow dish, whisk together milk and sour cream.

7. Re-line the second baking sheet and coat with cooking spray. Working with one piece at a time, dip tilapia in milk mixture and then carefully coat both sides in millet mixture. Transfer to baking sheet.

8. Bake for 15 minutes or until fish is cooked through. Serve with the potato chips.

PER SERVING | Calories: 360 | Fat: 12g | Protein: 24g | Sodium: 955mg | Fiber: 5g | Carbohydrates: 42g | Sugar: 3g

Summery Fish Stew

When summer evenings start to get chilly, set this soup simmering. Pair with a light garden salad, a crusty gluten-free bread, fresh butter, and a glass of Sauvignon Blanc.

INGREDIENTS | SERVES 6

2 slices raw bacon

1 cup sliced carrot

4 cups Seafood Stock (see recipe in Chapter 8)

½ cup dry white wine

1 (14.5-ounce) can fire-roasted diced tomatoes

1 bay leaf

1 teaspoon sea salt

¼ teaspoon freshly ground black pepper

2 small red potatoes, peeled and cut into 1" pieces

2 pounds raw white-fleshed fish fillets, cut into 2" pieces

1 cup cut green beans

1 cup corn kernels

½ cup Whipped Cream (see recipe in Chapter 14)

1 tablespoon chopped fresh parsley

1. Cook bacon in a large stockpot over medium heat. Transfer bacon to a paper towel–lined plate to cool.

2. To same pot, add carrots and sauté for 10 minutes over medium-low heat, stirring occasionally. Add stock, wine, tomatoes, bay leaf, salt, and pepper.

3. Bring just to a boil, then reduce heat and simmer for 20 minutes. Add potatoes and simmer uncovered 15 minutes. Add fish, beans, and corn; return to a simmer, stirring occasionally. Simmer uncovered 5 minutes. Remove from heat and let stand 5 minutes more, until fish is cooked through.

4. Remove and discard bay leaf. Chop and add in bacon. Stir in whipped cream.

5. Ladle stew into bowls, garnish with parsley, and serve.

PER SERVING | Calories: 414 | Fat: 15g | Protein: 36g | Sodium: 1,455mg | Fiber: 6g | Carbohydrates: 31g | Sugar: 9g

Feta Crab Cakes

For a beautiful presentation, serve these pretty crab cakes over a bed of greens, topped with roasted bell peppers and drizzled with Tzatziki Dressing (see recipe in Chapter 9).

INGREDIENTS | SERVES 4

5 slices gluten-free bread, toasted

½ teaspoon sea salt

⅛ teaspoon freshly ground black pepper

12 ounces lump cooked crabmeat

½ cup crumbled feta cheese

½ teaspoon dried basil

½ teaspoon dried oregano

½ teaspoon dried marjoram

½ teaspoon dried thyme

1 tablespoon lactose-free plain low-fat yogurt

1 large egg, beaten, divided

1. Preheat oven to 400°F. Line a baking sheet with parchment paper and brush with safflower oil.

2. Add toast, salt, and pepper to a food processor. Pulse until fine bread crumbs form.

3. In a large bowl, combine ⅓ cup bread crumbs, crabmeat, feta, basil, oregano, marjoram, thyme, yogurt, and 1 tablespoon beaten egg. Stir well to combine.

4. Place remaining beaten egg in a bowl. Place remaining bread crumbs in a separate shallow bowl. Create 8 equal round balls of crab mixture. Working with one ball at a time, flatten to a ½" disc, then coat in egg, followed by bread crumbs. Transfer to baking sheet.

5. Bake 10 minutes, then carefully turn each cake over and bake 10 minutes more.

PER SERVING | Calories: 270 | Fat: 7g | Protein: 26g | Sodium: 1,065mg | Fiber: 1g | Carbohydrates: 24g | Sugar: 2g

Bacon-Wrapped Maple Scallops

Easy to make, these scallops can make for an elegant dinner fare
or a talk-of-the-party hors d'oeuvre . . . you decide!

INGREDIENTS | SERVES 10

20 large sea scallops

10 slices bacon, halved

1 recipe Autumn's Glaze (see recipe in Chapter 9)

1. Preheat broiler and line a baking sheet with foil.

2. Wrap each scallop with a half slice of bacon; secure with a toothpick and transfer to baking sheet.

3. Broil 10–12 minutes, turning once, until bacon is fully cooked on all sides.

4. Drizzle glaze evenly over scallops and serve immediately.

PER SERVING | Calories: 186 | Fat: 14g | Protein: 9g | Sodium: 285mg | Fiber: 0g | Carbohydrates: 5g | Sugar: 4g

Grilled Halibut with Lemony Pesto

*Be sure to marinate the halibut for only 30 minutes. Any longer
and the citrus juices may start to "cook" your fish!*

INGREDIENTS | SERVES 4

1 tablespoon grapeseed oil

2 tablespoons freshly squeezed lemon juice, divided

2 teaspoons grated lemon zest, divided

½ teaspoon sea salt

¼ teaspoon freshly ground black pepper

4 (6-ounce) raw halibut steaks

½ cup Garden Pesto (see recipe in Chapter 9)

1. Whisk oil, 1 tablespoon lemon juice, 1 teaspoon zest, salt, and pepper in a large bowl. Add halibut and marinate for 30 minutes.

2. Add pesto, remaining juice, and remaining zest to a food processor. Pulse just until combined.

3. Heat a charcoal grill, gas grill, or broiler to 350°F. Grill or broil steaks, about 6 minutes per side until fish is cooked through.

4. Top fish with the lemony pesto and serve immediately.

PER SERVING | Calories: 356 | Fat: 20g | Protein: 39g | Sodium: 675mg | Fiber: 1g | Carbohydrates: 3g | Sugar: 0g

Cedar Planked Salmon

It's the ultimate flavor agent: Using a cedar plank to grill salmon imbues a woodsy, smoky taste and aroma into the dish.

INGREDIENTS | SERVES 4

Cedar grilling plank

1 tablespoon demerara sugar

1 teaspoon freshly ground tricolored peppercorns

¼ teaspoon sea salt

⅛ teaspoon pure vanilla extract

12-ounce raw salmon fillet

1. Prepare cedar plank by soaking in warm water for at least 1 hour.

2. In a small bowl, mix sugar, peppercorns, salt, and vanilla. Rub all over salmon and transfer, skin-side down, to prepared plank.

3. Heat a charcoal grill, gas grill, or broiler to 350°F. Grill or broil salmon, skin-side down on plank, for 15 minutes.

PER SERVING | Calories: 133 | Fat: 5g | Protein: 17g | Sodium: 185mg | Fiber: 0g | Carbohydrates: 4g | Sugar: 3g

Citrusy Swordfish Skewers

This sweet and savory marinade works just as well with tuna steak. For a complete light and simple supper, pair with Toasted Coconut Almond Millet (see recipe in Chapter 13).

INGREDIENTS | SERVES 4

2 medium oranges, peeled

4 (4-ounce) swordfish steaks

2 tablespoons Garlic-Infused Oil (see recipe in Chapter 9)

1 tablespoon orange juice

1 teaspoon dried oregano

½ teaspoon sea salt

1. Cut each orange into six equal parts. Cut swordfish into 2" cubes.

2. Combine oil, orange juice, oregano, and salt in a medium bowl. Whisk marinade; add fish and orange pieces. Toss to coat. Marinate for 60 minutes, tossing occasionally.

3. Skewer the swordfish and orange pieces in an alternating fish/fruit pattern.

4. Heat grill or broiler to medium. Grill or broil skewers for 15 minutes, turning once, until fish is cooked through. Serve immediately.

PER SERVING | Calories: 230 | Fat: 11g | Protein: 23g | Sodium: 395mg | Fiber: 2g | Carbohydrates: 9g | Sugar: 6g

Coconut Shrimp

Using unsweetened coconut not only makes this dish FODMAP-friendly, it also saves the sugar for the sauce. Serve with Kiwi Dipping Sauce (see recipe in Chapter 9).

INGREDIENTS | SERVES 4

1 slice gluten-free bread, toasted

½ cup unsweetened finely shredded coconut

⅛ teaspoon sea salt

1 large egg

⅛ teaspoon pure vanilla extract

16 large raw shrimp, peeled and deveined

Sweetened versus Unsweetened Coconut

While on the low-FODMAP diet, it is advisable to stick with unsweetened shredded coconut to avoid taking in any unwanted high-FODMAP ingredients. Because unsweetened coconut is drier, you may need to add a little extra water when swapping in unsweetened for sweetened in your own favorite recipes.

1. Preheat oven to 425°F. Line a baking sheet with foil and coat with coconut oil spray.

2. Add toast to food processor. Pulse until fine bread crumbs form.

3. In a flat dish, mix bread crumbs with coconut and salt.

4. In a small bowl, whisk together egg and vanilla.

5. Dip each shrimp into egg mixture, then into bread-crumb/coconut mixture. Transfer to baking sheet.

6. Bake for 5 minutes. Carefully turn each shrimp over and bake for 5 minutes more or until shrimp are fully cooked through. Serve immediately.

PER SERVING | Calories: 88 | Fat: 5g | Protein: 5g | Sodium: 160mg | Fiber: 1g | Carbohydrates: 6g | Sugar: 1g

Tilapia Piccata

You will not want to miss a lick of this "lemon from heaven" sauce—to be sure you don't, serve with the Umami Risotto (see recipe in Chapter 13).

INGREDIENTS | SERVES 6

¼ cup dry white wine

3 tablespoons freshly squeezed lemon juice, preferably Meyer

1 teaspoon fresh lemon zest

2 tablespoons capers, rinsed, drained

¼ cup sweet rice flour, divided

½ teaspoon sea salt

¼ teaspoon freshly ground black pepper

4 (6-ounce) pieces tilapia fillets

1 tablespoon Garlic-Infused Oil (see recipe in Chapter 9)

1 teaspoon butter

1 tablespoon chopped fresh parsley

1. In a small bowl, whisk wine, lemon juice, zest, and capers.

2. Reserve 1 teaspoon flour and set aside. Mix remaining flour with salt and pepper on a plate. Dip fish into flour.

3. Heat oil over medium heat in a large skillet. Add fish and cook 2–3 minutes per side. When fish is cooked through, remove from pan.

4. Add wine mixture and reserved flour to pan and cook 1 minute, whisking constantly. Remove from heat and stir in butter.

5. Top fish with the sauce, garnish with parsley, and serve immediately.

PER SERVING | Calories: 168 | Fat: 5g | Protein: 23g | Sodium: 342mg | Fiber: 0g | Carbohydrates: 6g | Sugar: 0g

CHAPTER 13

Vegetarian Mains, Sides, and Salads

Basic Salad Dressing

Make this salad dressing once a week so that you have it readily available for side salads and quick lunches. Dressing can be stored in the refrigerator for approximately one week. Remember to take it out of the refrigerator to warm a bit before use.

INGREDIENTS | MAKES 1¾ CUPS

½ cup red wine vinegar

1 tablespoon Dijon mustard

1 cup extra-virgin olive oil

½ teaspoon dried thyme

Juice of 1 medium lemon

1 tablespoon pure maple syrup

¼ teaspoon sea salt

¼ teaspoon freshly ground black pepper

Combine all ingredients in a bowl and whisk until emulsified.

PER SERVING (2 TABLESPOONS) | Calories: 143 | Fat: 15g | Protein: 0g | Sodium: 55mg | Fiber: 0g | Carbohydrates: 1g | Sugar: 1g

Arugula Salad with Melon

This beautiful salad can dress up an ordinary dinner, or shine at a formal affair. Arugula can be a little bitter, but the juices from the melon add a nice touch of sweetness that mellows out the flavor.

INGREDIENTS | SERVES 4

¼ cup chopped pecans

3 ounces arugula

¼ cantaloupe, peeled, seeded, and cut into 1" pieces

4 tablespoons Basic Salad Dressing (see recipe in this chapter)

1. Preheat broiler. Place pecans on a rimmed baking sheet and toast for 3 minutes.

2. Combine all other ingredients in salad bowl. Garnish with toasted pecans.

PER SERVING | Calories: 125 | Fat: 12g | Protein: 1g | Sodium: 15mg | Fiber: 1g | Carbohydrates: 5g | Sugar: 4g

Arugula for Health

Arugula, also known as rocket lettuce, is a nutrition powerhouse. The compounds that add to its bitter flavor contribute to the fact that arugula has more antioxidants than most other lettuces. Among other things, arugula is high in vitamins A, C, K, and folate.

Ginger Sesame Salad Dressing

Use this dressing to practice mindfulness, as you savor all of the various flavors on your tongue. This dressing can be used for any salad, but pairs beautifully with Mixed Greens with Mandarin Oranges (see recipe in this chapter).

INGREDIENTS | MAKES 1 CUP

½ cup extra-virgin olive oil

¼ cup rice wine vinegar

2 tablespoons gluten-free tamari

2 tablespoons demerara sugar

1 teaspoon sesame oil

1" fresh ginger, peeled, minced

Blend all ingredients until smooth. Dressing can be stored for one week in the refrigerator. Bring to room temperature before serving.

PER SERVING (2 TABLESPOONS) | Calories: 140 | Fat: 14g | Protein: 0g | Sodium: 225mg | Fiber: 0g | Carbohydrates: 3g | Sugar: 3g

Ginger for Health

Ginger has long been prized for its health benefits. It is known to soothe nausea, it supports the immune system, and it has strong anti-inflammatory effects. Fresh ginger can be stored in your refrigerator for up to three weeks or in the freezer for up to six months.

Mixed Greens with Mandarin Oranges

This recipe uses only lettuce types from the allowed list. Once you have completed the Elimination Phase of the diet you may find that you are able to tolerate the variety of greens found in the more convenient spring mix packages. Top the salad with Ginger Sesame Salad Dressing (see recipe in this chapter).

INGREDIENTS | SERVES 4

2 cups baby spinach leaves

2 cups arugula

2 cups red coral lettuce

2 cups butter lettuce

1 (15-ounce) can mandarin oranges in light syrup, drained, rinsed well

2 tablespoons sliced almonds

Place greens in a bowl. Top with mandarin oranges and almonds.

PER SERVING | Calories: 69 | Fat: 2g | Protein: 3g | Sodium: 26mg | Fiber: 3g | Carbohydrates: 12g | Sugar: 9g

Garlicky Smashed Potatoes

In this recipe, the browned butter, infused with garlic, adds richness and flavor to an easy potato side dish.

4 medium red potatoes, cut in 1" cubes

4 tablespoons butter

4 garlic cloves, peeled, slightly smashed

½ cup lactose-free whole milk

1 teaspoon sea salt

½ teaspoon freshly ground black pepper

No More Plain Baked Potatoes!

As you experience symptom relief from following the low-FODMAP diet, you will find that you no longer have to restrict yourself to eating plain baked potatoes in order to feel well. Russet and red potatoes are allowed in all phases of the diet, as are sweet potatoes if you keep your portion size to ½ cup.

1. In a medium stockpot, cover potatoes with water and bring to a boil over high heat. Reduce heat to medium-low and simmer uncovered 20 minutes, or until potatoes are very tender.

2. While potatoes are simmering, melt butter in a small skillet over medium heat. Add garlic and swirl.

3. When butter starts to brown, turn off heat. Remove and discard garlic, reserving butter. Set aside to cool.

4. Once cool, add milk to the butter and stir to combine.

5. When potatoes are fully cooked, use a potato masher to render a smashed consistency. Add butter mixture and stir to combine. Season with salt and pepper and serve.

PER SERVING | Calories: 275 | Fat: 13g | Protein: 5g | Sodium: 615mg | Fiber: 4g | Carbohydrates: 37g | Sugar: 4g

Garlic-Infused Spinach

The spinach in this recipe can be swapped out for any low-FODMAP green, including bok choy, green cabbage, kale, or Swiss chard.

INGREDIENTS | SERVES 4

1 tablespoon Garlic-Infused Oil (see recipe in Chapter 9)

4 cups packed baby spinach leaves

1 tablespoon red wine vinegar

⅛ teaspoon sea salt

1. Heat oil over medium heat in a large skillet. Add spinach and stir quickly.

2. Add vinegar and stir until all spinach is just wilted. Season with salt and serve warm.

PER SERVING | Calories: 39 | Fat: 3g | Protein: 1g | Sodium: 97mg | Fiber: 1g | Carbohydrates: 1g | Sugar: 0g

The Importance of Greens

As you follow the low-FODMAP diet, it would be good to increase your intake of green, leafy vegetables to make up for the loss of the high-FODMAP-containing vegetables you will be avoiding. Greens are a great source of dietary fiber and provide you with many vitamins, minerals, and phytochemicals.

String Beans and Sweet Potato Fries

Mixing the string beans in with the sweet potatoes allows you to feel like you are having a full serving of "fries" while keeping your intake of sweet potatoes at a FODMAP-friendly level.

INGREDIENTS | SERVES 6

2 medium sweet potatoes, peeled

2 tablespoons extra-virgin olive oil, divided

¼ teaspoon sea salt, divided

1 pound green beans, trimmed

1. Heat oven to 400°F.

2. Cut ends off sweet potatoes. Slice each sweet potato lengthwise at ½" intervals. Cut each slice into ½" strips.

3. Place sweet potatoes onto a rimmed baking sheet. Add 1 tablespoon oil and stir to coat. Season with ⅛ teaspoon of salt. Try to arrange potato slices so they are not touching.

4. Place string beans on a second rimmed baking sheet. Coat with remaining oil and season with remaining salt.

5. Place both trays in oven and roast for 30 minutes, stirring every 10 minutes.

6. Mix together and serve.

PER SERVING | Calories: 100 | Fat: 5g | Protein: 2g | Sodium: 125mg | Fiber: 3g | Carbohydrates: 14g | Sugar: 4g

Bok Choy with Parmesan

For your digestive and overall health it is important to eat lots of green leafy vegetables. The bok choy in this recipe can be swapped out for any low-FODMAP green, such as kale, spinach, or Swiss chard.

INGREDIENTS | SERVES 4

1 tablespoon Garlic-Infused Oil (see recipe in Chapter 9)

1 head bok choy, trimmed and roughly cut

¼ cup white wine

Juice of 1 medium lemon

1 tablespoon grated Parmesan cheese

¼ teaspoon freshly ground black pepper

How to Trim Bok Choy

Bok choy is not nearly as mysterious as it seems. To trim, cut off the root end about 1" from the bottom and discard. Rinse the bok choy well, making sure to get in between the leaves. Cut the leaves off of the stems and chop roughly. Cut the stem into bite-sized pieces. If you have purchased the more tender baby bok choy, there is no need to cook the stems separate from the leaves.

1. Heat oil in a large skillet over medium heat. Add bok choy stems to pan and sauté for 1 minute. Add leaves and cook for an additional minute.

2. Add white wine, cover, and cook for 5 minutes. Remove cover and cook 1 minute more, boiling off the wine.

3. Turn off heat. Add lemon juice, Parmesan cheese, and pepper and stir.

PER SERVING | Calories: 78 | Fat: 4g | Protein: 4g | Sodium: 167mg | Fiber: 2g | Carbohydrates: 6g | Sugar: 3g

Bok Choy with Roasted Carrots

This is sure to become a low-FODMAP favorite—colorful enough to serve on a holiday or special occasion, but easy enough for a weeknight side.

1. Heat oven to 375°F. Place carrots on a rimmed baking sheet and toss with 1 tablespoon olive oil, rosemary, salt, and pepper. Roast 20 minutes, stirring once.

2. Place bok choy on top of carrots. Drizzle with remaining tablespoon of olive oil. Continue roasting 10 minutes more, stirring once.

PER SERVING | Calories: 90 | Fat: 5g | Protein: 3g | Sodium: 240mg | Fiber: 4g | Carbohydrates: 10g | Sugar: 5g

Kale with Toasted Walnuts

Although this dish makes a side dish for four, feel free to whip this up for lunch and eat it all by yourself!

INGREDIENTS | SERVES 4

1 tablespoon Garlic-Infused Oil (see recipe in Chapter 9)

1 bunch kale, stems removed, coarsely chopped

¼ cup water

⅓ cup chopped walnuts

Juice of 1 medium lemon

⅛ teaspoon freshly ground black pepper

1. Heat oil in a large skillet over medium-high heat. Add kale to pan and sauté for 1 minute until the leaves begin to wilt.

2. Reduce heat to medium-low and add ¼ cup water. Cover and cook for 8 minutes, stirring occasionally.

3. While kale is cooking, preheat broiler for 5 minutes. Place the walnuts in a rimmed baking pan and broil for 4 minutes or until toasted and fragrant.

4. When kale has finished cooking, remove the pan from the heat. Stir in walnuts, lemon juice, and black pepper.

PER SERVING | Calories: 129 | Fat: 10g | Protein: 4g | Sodium: 30mg | Fiber: 2g | Carbohydrates: 8g | Sugar: 0g

Roasted Vegetables

This recipe is sure to be a favorite for all as they see how sweet roasted vegetables can be! You can also use these vegetables to create a warming soup (see Roasted Vegetable Soup in Chapter 8).

INGREDIENTS | SERVES 6

1 large butternut squash, peeled, seeded, and cut into 1" chunks

2 medium eggplants, cut into 1" chunks

1 pound carrots, peeled and cut into 1" chunks

1 pound parsnips, peeled and cut into 1" chunks

4 tablespoons extra-virgin olive oil, divided

2 tablespoons dried thyme, divided

½ teaspoon, sea salt, divided

½ teaspoon freshly ground black pepper, divided

1. Heat oven to 425°F. Place squash, eggplant, carrots, and parsnips on two rimmed baking sheets. Toss each sheet with 2 tablespoons olive oil, 1 tablespoon of thyme, and ¼ teaspoon each of salt and pepper.

2. Roast vegetables for 45 minutes, stirring every 15 minutes.

PER SERVING | Calories: 245 | Fat: 10g | Protein: 4g | Sodium: 260mg | Fiber: 14g | Carbohydrates: 40g | Sugar: 13g

Swiss Chard with Yellow Squash

Here is another way to get in your veggies for the day. This bright, colorful side dish can also double as a quick, super-nutritious lunch.

INGREDIENTS | SERVES 4

⅛ cup sliced almonds

1 tablespoon extra-virgin olive oil

2 medium yellow squash, diced

⅛ teaspoon ground red pepper

1 bunch Swiss chard

¼ cup water

⅛ cup freshly grated Parmesan cheese

Swiss Chard

Swiss chard is sometimes called "rainbow chard," as it comes in the most beautiful colors. As you make this dish, be aware of all of the amazing phytonutrients—health-filled plant chemicals—that you will be putting into your body.

1. Preheat broiler. Toast almonds in a rimmed pan for 3 minutes. Set aside to cool.

2. Heat oil in a large skillet over medium heat. Add squash and ground red pepper. Sauté 5 minutes.

3. Add Swiss chard to pan, stirring for 1 minute. Add ¼ cup water, cover, and cook for 5 minutes. Uncover and cook 3 minutes more, stirring occasionally.

4. Remove from heat. Top with almonds and Parmesan cheese before serving.

PER SERVING | Calories: 77 | Fat: 6g | Protein: 3g | Sodium: 134mg | Fiber: 1g | Carbohydrates: 4g | Sugar: 2g

Toasted Coconut Almond Millet

Missing couscous on a low-FODMAP diet? Give delicious, versatile millet a try. You are sure to love its sweet, nutty flavor.

INGREDIENTS | SERVES 4

1 cup millet

1½ cups filtered water

¼ cup orange juice

⅛ teaspoon pure vanilla extract

⅛ teaspoon freshly ground black pepper

½ teaspoon sea salt

½ cup sliced almonds

¼ cup shredded unsweetened coconut

1 teaspoon pure maple syrup

Meet Millet

Here is another gluten-free grain that you will want to get to know as you follow the low-FODMAP diet. Millet is packed with fiber. It is also a good source of protein, B vitamins, copper, magnesium, manganese, and phosphorus. Millet can be used for baking or cooked like rice.

1. Heat a medium saucepan over medium heat. Add millet and sauté 2–3 minutes or until fragrant.

2. Add water, orange juice, vanilla, pepper, and salt. Bring just to a boil and then reduce heat to low. Simmer, covered, 25–30 minutes or until all water is absorbed.

3. Meanwhile, preheat broiler. Line a baking sheet with foil. Toss almonds with coconut on the baking sheet. Spray with coconut oil spray and toss to coat. Broil 1–2 minutes or until mixture starts to turn light brown. Remove from broiler, transfer to a bowl, and toss with maple syrup.

4. When millet is cooked, fluff with a fork. Divide evenly among serving plates and sprinkle with toasted coconut mixture.

PER SERVING | Calories: 287 | Fat: 10g | Protein: 8g | Sodium: 300mg | Fiber: 6g | Carbohydrates: 43g | Sugar: 3g

Veggie "Meatballs"

Taking advantage of eggplant's naturally meaty texture, you can create a satisfying alternative to traditional meatballs. This recipe pairs well with Traditional Tomato Sauce (see recipe in Chapter 9).

INGREDIENTS | SERVES 4

Skin from 1 medium eggplant, insides discarded or repurposed

1 cup baby carrots

1 cup canned brown lentils, drained and rinsed

2 slices gluten-free toast

1 medium egg

½ cup grated Parmesan cheese

1 teaspoon dried basil

1 teaspoon dried oregano

½ teaspoon sea salt

¼ teaspoon freshly ground black pepper

½ teaspoon psyllium husks

1. Process eggplant skin, carrots, and lentils in a food processor to a coarse consistency.

2. Add toast, egg, cheese, basil, oregano, salt, pepper, and psyllium. Pulse until combined (and large chunks of bread are no longer visible).

3. Preheat broiler. Form mixture into 16 equally sized balls and place on a foil-lined baking sheet. Broil for 5–8 minutes, until tops are evenly browned.

4. Remove sheet. Carefully turn balls over and broil for another 3–5 minutes, until browned on all sides and insides are fully cooked. Serve.

PER SERVING | Calories: 173 | Fat: 5g | Protein: 12g | Sodium: 594mg | Fiber: 5g | Carbohydrates: 19g | Sugar: 2g

Umami Risotto

Sadly, mushrooms are not allowed on the low-FODMAP diet. But this risotto captures their umami flavor with a drizzle of aromatic white truffle oil just prior to serving.

INGREDIENTS | SERVES 4

2 tablespoons Garlic-Infused Oil (see recipe in Chapter 9)

1 cup Arborio rice

½ cup dry white wine

6 cups Vegetable Stock (see recipe in Chapter 8)

½ cup grated Parmesan cheese

1 teaspoon white truffle oil

What Does Umami Mean?

Our tastes of bitter, salty, sour, and sweet are rounded out by umami. It is typically described as savory; a strong and pleasant flavor detected by the taste buds in our tongues. Slowing down to focus on all five senses as you eat can not only enhance your enjoyment, but is also important for optimal digestion.

1. Heat oil in a large, high-sided skillet over medium-low heat. Stir in rice and sauté for 5 minutes.

2. Add wine and stir until fully absorbed.

3. Add 1 cup of stock, increase heat to medium-high, stir, and bring to a boil. Lower heat to medium-low and simmer uncovered, stirring often, until broth is absorbed. Add more broth, 1 cup at a time, simmering uncovered and stirring often, until all broth is absorbed. This process should take about 25 minutes from start to finish.

4. Stir in cheese, drizzle with oil, and serve.

PER SERVING | Calories: 455 | Fat: 16g | Protein: 17g | Sodium: 705mg | Fiber: 1g | Carbohydrates: 54g | Sugar: 6g

Root-a-Burgers

You can't put high-FODMAP mushrooms on top of these burgers, but a drizzle of black truffle oil before and after grilling provides a similar—more dramatic—earthy flavor.

INGREDIENTS | SERVES 6

2 medium parsnips, peeled and cut into ½" rounds

2 medium carrots, peeled and cut into ½" rounds

1 teaspoon grapeseed oil

2 teaspoons salt, divided

½ teaspoon freshly ground black pepper, divided

2 slices gluten-free bread, toasted

1 cup canned lentils, drained and well rinsed

1 large egg

1 cup freshly grated Parmesan cheese

1 teaspoon black truffle oil

What Is Truffle Oil?

Truffles are a type of fungi, often found near the roots of trees; not all are edible. Truffle oil adds the taste of truffles to cooking. White truffle oil provides a fairly light, herby taste while black truffle oil has a stronger, earthy taste. Some truffle oils are made from synthetic ingredients; true oil is more expensive. Although neither one has been specifically tested for FODMAP content, typically oils are low in FODMAPs.

1. Preheat oven to 400°F. Line a baking sheet with parchment paper.

2. In a large bowl, toss parsnips and carrots with grapeseed oil, 1 teaspoon salt, and ¼ teaspoon pepper. Spread on baking sheet and bake for 30 minutes. Set aside to cool.

3. In a food processor, pulse toast to a crumb consistency. Transfer to a bowl.

4. Add roasted vegetables to food processor and pulse until there are no major lumps. Add remaining salt and pepper, bread crumbs, lentils, egg, cheese, and 1 teaspoon truffle oil. Pulse to combine.

5. Transfer to a workspace and form six equal patty rounds.

6. Refrigerate patties for 12–24 hours before grilling or broiling on an oiled surface.

PER SERVING | Calories: 200 | Fat: 8g | Protein: 12g | Sodium: 1,185mg | Fiber: 5g | Carbohydrates: 20g | Sugar: 3g

Tofu Stir-Fry

Here is a low-FODMAP version of a classic vegetarian standby.
Serve over brown rice for a satisfying lunch or dinner.

INGREDIENTS | SERVES 6

⅔ cup gluten-free tamari

2 tablespoons rice wine vinegar

¼ cup maple syrup

1 (14-ounce) package firm tofu, drained, pressed, and cut into 1" cubes

2 tablespoons extra-virgin olive oil

1" piece fresh ginger, peeled, minced

1 medium red bell pepper, seeded and sliced

3 medium carrots, peeled and cut into 2" matchsticks

2 cups broccoli florets (from 2 stalks)

2 cups thinly sliced common (green) cabbage (approximately ¼ of whole)

½ cup plus 1 tablespoon water, divided

2 teaspoons cornstarch

How to Press Tofu

Pressing tofu rids it of excess moisture, which improves its ability to soak up the flavors of its surrounding sauce. Cover a cookie sheet with a kitchen towel, with two paper towels placed on top. Add the tofu and cover with two additional paper towels, topped with another kitchen towel and another cookie sheet. Place some heavy cookbooks on top. Tofu can be used after a 30-minute press.

1. In large bowl, stir together tamari, vinegar, and maple syrup. Add tofu and marinate for 30 minutes.

2. Heat oil in large skillet over medium-high heat. Stir-fry ginger for 1 minute. Add bell pepper, carrots, broccoli, and cabbage. Stir-fry for 4 minutes.

3. With slotted spoon, remove tofu from marinade and add to vegetables, reserving marinade. Stir-fry for 1 minute, stirring carefully.

4. Add ½ cup water to skillet. Cover and cook for 4 minutes.

5. In a small bowl, mix cornstarch with 1 tablespoon water. Add to reserved marinade.

6. When vegetables have finished steaming, add marinade and cook for 5 minutes, until sauce has thickened.

PER SERVING | Calories: 172 | Fat: 7g | Protein: 8g | Sodium: 1,650mg | Fiber: 3g | Carbohydrates: 22g | Sugar: 13g

Confetti Corn

It's easy to eat a rainbow when this dish is part of your menu. Fresh corn and basil turn this colorful side into a real taste of summer.

INGREDIENTS | SERVES 4

2 medium ears corn, shucked and cooked
1 tablespoon butter
½ cup finely diced red bell pepper
½ cup finely diced yellow bell pepper
½ cup finely diced orange bell pepper
½ cup finely diced green bell pepper
½ teaspoon sea salt
⅛ teaspoon ground red pepper
¼ cup chopped fresh basil leaves

1. Cut kernels off cobs into a medium bowl.

2. Melt butter in a large skillet over medium-low heat.

3. Add bell peppers, salt, and pepper; sauté, stirring occasionally, for 8–10 minutes.

4. Add corn kernels to pepper mixture and sauté for 3–5 minutes more, stirring occasionally.

5. Transfer to a serving dish and garnish with basil.

PER SERVING | Calories: 110 | Fat: 4g | Protein: 3g | Sodium: 300mg | Fiber: 3g | Carbohydrates: 19g | Sugar: 5g

CHAPTER 14

Desserts

Dark Chocolate Dip

This decadent dip can be served warm as a fondue or used to coat low-FODMAP berries, gluten-free pretzels, or potato chips. Simply drizzle the dip onto your treats, then transfer to the refrigerator until firm.

INGREDIENTS | MAKES ¾ CUP

½ cup unrefined coconut oil, liquefied

½ cup raw cacao powder

1 tablespoon pure maple syrup

½ cup dark chocolate chips

Health Benefits of Cacao

All chocolate products are made from cacao beans. Cacao is considered a super-food as it is filled with antioxidants, flavonoids, vitamins, minerals (particularly iron), and soluble fiber. You probably already know that it is mood elevating, but you may not know that cacao supports the immune system, promotes cardiovascular health, and is anti-inflammatory.

1. Warm coconut oil in a small saucepan over low heat. Whisk in cacao powder and maple syrup.

2. Add chocolate chips and stir to melt. Remove from heat and serve or use as a coating.

PER SERVING (2 TABLESPOONS) | Calories: 250 | Fat: 23g | Protein: 2g | Sodium: 3mg | Fiber: 3g | Carbohydrates: 15g | Sugar: 10g

Whipped Cream

Add a teaspoon of ground turbinado sugar to sweeten, if desired. Store in fridge for up to three days.

INGREDIENTS | MAKES 1½ CUPS

1 pint heavy whipping cream

Sugar and the Low-FODMAP Diet

Good news if you have a sweet tooth! Sugar, in the form of sucrose, is allowed in moderation in all phases of the diet, as it is made up of equal parts of glucose and fructose. This includes table sugar, powdered sugar, and brown sugar, as well as the unrefined raw sugars, (turbinado, demerara, or muscavado), coconut sugar, and maple syrup, that were chosen for the recipes in this book due to their higher nutrient profiles.

1. Place a metal mixing bowl into the refrigerator for 10 minutes.

2. Remove bowl, add cream, and whip on medium-high speed for 3–5 minutes, or until stiff peaks form.

PER SERVING (2 TABLESPOONS) | Calories: 138 | Fat: 15g | Protein: 1g | Sodium: 15mg | Fiber: 0g | Carbohydrates: 1g | Sugar: 0g

Caramel Sauce

Here is a healthier (and diet-approved) alternative to melting packaged caramels. Use this sauce as a dip or sundae topping or incorporate it into recipes, such as Peppermint Patties and Salted Caramel Fondue, both of which can be found in this chapter.

INGREDIENTS | MAKES ⅓ CUP

⅓ cup demerara sugar

⅓ cup filtered water

1 teaspoon lemon juice

1 tablespoon unrefined coconut oil, liquefied

1. Grind sugar in a coffee grinder.

2. Combine sugar, ⅓ cup water, and lemon juice in a small saucepan over medium heat.

3. Bring just to a boil, then lower heat to a bubbling simmer. Stir constantly for 10 minutes, until sauce starts to thicken.

4. Remove from heat and stir in coconut oil.

PER SERVING (1 TABLESPOON) | Calories: 75 | Fat: 3g | Protein: 0g | Sodium: 0mg | Fiber: 0g | Carbohydrates: 14g | Sugar: 13g

Salted Caramel Fondue

Ideas for dipping treats include whole strawberries, banana slices, Brazil nuts, gluten-free pretzel rods, broken-up dark chocolate bars, and cubes of Banana Sheet Cake (see recipe in this chapter). The fondue makes a great sundae, cooled and drizzled over gluten-free, lactose-free ice cream.

INGREDIENTS | MAKES 1 CUP

⅓ cup Caramel Sauce (see recipe in this chapter)

⅛ teaspoon pure vanilla extract

½ teaspoon sea salt

¼ teaspoon arrowroot powder

½ cup Whipped Cream (see recipe in this chapter)

1. In a small saucepan over medium-low heat, whisk Caramel Sauce with vanilla, salt, and arrowroot powder. Fold in cream.

2. Transfer to a fondue pot and serve.

PER SERVING (2 TABLESPOONS) | Calories: 100 | Fat: 7g | Protein: 0g | Sodium: 150mg | Fiber: 0g | Carbohydrates: 9g | Sugar: 8g

Health Benefits of Pure Vanilla Extract

Pure vanilla extract may cost more than imitation, but the extra expense is well worth it. Imitation vanilla extract contains artificial flavorings and chemicals, whereas pure vanilla extract contains small amounts of vitamins and minerals. Your taste buds and your body will thank you for choosing the pure version.

Peppermint Patties

Satisfy your sweet tooth with one of these small candy treats. You can experiment with different flavors by subbing in vanilla or almond extract for the peppermint.

INGREDIENTS | SERVES 8

¼ cup Caramel Sauce (see recipe in this chapter)

¼ teaspoon peppermint extract, divided

2 teaspoons arrowroot powder

1 cup Dark Chocolate Dip (see recipe in this chapter)

Peppermint for GI Health

Peppermint oil has strong support as an antispasmodic that eases abdominal pain from IBS. Peppermint is also thought to reduce indigestion, dyspepsia, gas, and bloating. The positive effects of peppermint are thought to come from menthol; thus, you can benefit from it in any form— oil, extract, or tea.

1. Clear enough space in the freezer to fit a metal mini-muffin pan laid flat.

2. In a small bowl, combine Caramel Sauce with ⅛ teaspoon extract and arrowroot powder. Set aside to thicken, about 20 minutes.

3. In a small saucepan, warm Chocolate Dip. Remove from heat and stir in remaining extract.

4. Spoon 1 heaping teaspoon Chocolate Dip into each of 8 cups in a mini-muffin pan. Set remaining dip aside. Carefully lay pan flat in freezer. Freeze for 10 minutes or until chocolate is completely firm.

5. Leave chocolate in the pan. Top each with ½ teaspoon peppermint/caramel mixture. Gently spread mixture in even circles, leaving a border of chocolate around each edge. Top evenly with another heaping teaspoon of Chocolate Dip, so all of the peppermint mixture is covered. Carefully return pan to freezer. Freeze for at least 20 minutes.

6. Remove pan from freezer, turn it over on a clean workspace, and firmly tap till all candies fall out. Transfer to an airtight container and store in refrigerator.

PER SERVING | Calories: 240 | Fat: 19g | Protein: 1.5g | Sodium: 3mg | Fiber: 2g | Carbohydrates: 20g | Sugar: 16g

Corn Flour Tartlets

This casually elegant raw-foods dessert is great for summer entertaining. Crusts can be plated up to a day ahead, then topped with whipped cream and berries just before serving.

INGREDIENTS | SERVES 4

½ cup cornmeal

1¼ cups gluten-free oat flour

½ teaspoon sea salt

2 tablespoons turbinado sugar

¼ cup solid unrefined coconut oil

½ cup Whipped Cream (see recipe in this chapter)

2 cups Strawberry Tart Filling (see recipe in this chapter)

1. Cut four 4" × 4" squares out of parchment paper, and one 8" × 8" square of waxed paper.

2. In a food processor, pulse to combine cornmeal, flour, salt, and sugar. Add oil and pulse continuously until mixture resembles tiny pebbles. Transfer dough to workspace and form into a disc with your hands. Divide dough into 4 equal parts.

3. Lay 1 square of parchment on a clean workspace. Place ¼ of the dough in the paper's center. Top with sheet of waxed paper and roll dough between the papers into a thin crust. Remove waxed paper.

4. Using a butter knife, trim the crust into a 3" × 3" square centered on the parchment paper. Carefully transfer parchment with dough to a dessert plate.

5. Add scraps to next quarter of dough and repeat to fill 4 dessert plates.

6. Spread 2 tablespoons Whipped Cream onto each dough square. Top with ½ cup Strawberry Tart Filling and serve.

PER SERVING | Calories: 500 | Fat: 29g | Protein: 8g | Sodium: 315mg | Fiber: 5g | Carbohydrates: 55g | Sugar: 15g

Strawberry Tart Filling

This recipe requires fresh berries, not frozen. Feel free to substitute or mix and match any variety of low-FODMAP berries, depending on taste preference and what's available at market.

INGREDIENTS | MAKES 2 CUPS

3 cups hulled strawberries, divided
1 tablespoon turbinado sugar
½ teaspoon balsamic vinegar

1. Purée 1 cup berries in a food processor. Slice remaining berries in half, leaving the smallest berries whole.

2. In a large bowl, mix sliced berries with purée and toss with sugar and vinegar.

3. Set aside to macerate (soften) for 30 minutes, stirring once or twice.

PER SERVING (½ CUP) | Calories: 47 | Fat: 0g | Protein: 1g | Sodium: 1mg | Fiber: 2g | Carbohydrates: 12g | Sugar: 8g

Candied Ginger Frosting

Most frosting recipes call for the use of confectioners' sugar—also a FODMAP-friendly choice. This one uses the slightly healthier turbinado sugar. In a semi-powdered state, the turbinado provides a unique candy-like crunch.

INGREDIENTS | LIGHTLY FROSTS 12 CUPCAKES

½ cup turbinado sugar

3 tablespoons butter, softened

3 tablespoons unrefined coconut oil, softened

¼ teaspoon freshly grated ginger

2 tablespoons Whipped Cream (see recipe in this chapter)

1. Add sugar to a coffee grinder in ¼-cup batches and process to a powdered state.

2. Cream powdered sugar, butter, oil, ginger, and whipped cream in a mixer until smooth.

PER SERVING (1 TABLESPOON) | Calories: 92 | Fat: 7g | Protein: 0g | Sodium: 1mg | Fiber: 0mg | Carbohydrates: 8g | Sugar: 8g

Sugar Tips

For both a healthy and a low-FODMAP diet, you will want to keep your sugar intake low. One way to do this is to use frosting as a decoration, rather than a heavy coat. Cakes can be modified into cupcakes for built-in portion control. Last, it is always sweet to split a dessert with someone you love!

Gingerbread Cupcakes

To achieve a classic gingerbread flavor, this recipe relies on pumpkin pie spice. Blends may vary a bit by brand, but most contain cinnamon, nutmeg, allspice, and ginger. Sneaking vegetables like eggplants into your baked goods not only ups nutrient and fiber values—it also adds moisture to often-dry gluten-free baked goods.

INGREDIENTS | SERVES 8

2 cups diced, peeled eggplant

1¼ cups all-purpose, gluten-free flour

¼ cup buckwheat flour

1 teaspoon gluten-free baking powder

½ teaspoon baking soda

⅛ teaspoon sea salt

1 tablespoon pumpkin pie spice

1 teaspoon white wine vinegar

1 tablespoon lactose-free milk

1 tablespoon blackstrap molasses

¼ cup muscovado sugar

½ cup pure maple syrup

1 large egg

¼ cup liquefied unrefined coconut oil

What Is Muscovado Sugar?

Muscovado is a sugar that's slightly healthier than most refined dark brown sugars commonly carried in stores today. Like turbinado and demerara sugar, it's minimally processed—but unlike those two it carries a strong molasses flavor. You can use muscovado sugar in place of dark brown sugar in equal amounts.

1. Heat oven to 350°F. Prepare a muffin pan with coconut oil spray or liners.

2. Process eggplant in a food processor. Transfer to a strainer over sink and squeeze to remove most of its liquid.

3. In a large bowl, mix flours, baking powder, baking soda, salt, and pumpkin pie spice.

4. In a small bowl, whisk together vinegar and milk.

5. In a mixer, blend molasses, sugar, maple syrup, egg, and coconut oil. By hand, stir in milk mixture. Add liquid mixture to flour mixture and eggplant, stirring gently just until combined. Do not overmix. Divide batter evenly in muffin pan.

6. Bake 18–20 minutes or until a toothpick inserted and removed from center remains clean.

PER SERVING | Calories: 160 | Fat: 5g | Protein: 2g | Sodium: 138mg | Fiber: 1g | Carbohydrates: 27g | Sugar: 14g

Banana Sheet Cake

For a special touch, decorate this cake with frosting. Make Candied Ginger Frosting (see recipe in this chapter), but substitute ¼ teaspoon of pure vanilla extract for the ginger. Fill a pastry bag with the frosting and draw some pretty wavy lines atop the cake.

INGREDIENTS | SERVES 12

3 medium ripe bananas, peeled
½ cup liquefied unrefined coconut oil
1 tablespoon blackstrap molasses
1 teaspoon pure vanilla extract
¾ cup demerara sugar
¼ cup lactose-free milk
2 large eggs
2¼ cups all-purpose, gluten-free flour
1 teaspoon gluten-free baking powder
½ teaspoon baking soda
⅛ teaspoon sea salt

Blackstrap Molasses and the Low-FODMAP Diet

Be careful with which molasses you choose. Some kinds of molasses are made with high-FODMAP ingredients. Blackstrap molasses is the liquid that is left over when sugar is extracted from sugar cane. Because it comes directly from the cane, it retains the benefits of the plant's vitamins and minerals. Limit your serving size of blackstrap molasses to 1 tablespoon.

1. Preheat oven to 375°F. Line a 13" × 9" baking dish with parchment paper and spray with coconut oil spray.

2. In mixer, blend bananas, oil, molasses, vanilla, sugar, and milk. Add eggs; mix until combined.

3. In a large bowl, whisk together flour, baking powder, baking soda, and salt. Drizzle banana mixture over the flour mixture, stirring gently just until combined. Do not over-stir.

4. Pour batter evenly into prepared dish. Bake 20 minutes or until a toothpick inserted and removed from center remains clean.

PER SERVING | Calories: 260 | Fat: 10g | Protein: 4g | Sodium: 130mg | Fiber: 1g | Carbohydrates: 38g | Sugar: 17g

Molten Chocolate Cakes

Serve these rich chocolate rice-pudding cakes warm in their ramekins. Place on a saucer, alongside a scoop of gluten-free, lactose-free vanilla bean ice cream.

INGREDIENTS | SERVES 6

2 cups cooked black rice

½ cup ripe avocado

½ cup liquefied unrefined coconut oil

1 cup raw cacao powder

¾ cup pure maple syrup

2 teaspoons pure vanilla extract

2 large eggs

¾ cup all-purpose gluten-free flour

1 teaspoon baking powder

½ teaspoon sea salt

½ cup dark chocolate chips

Chocolate and the Low-FODMAP Diet

For baking and hot chocolate you may safely consume up to 3 heaping tablespoons of cocoa or raw cacao powder (sometimes the terms are used interchangeably, but sometimes there are slight differences—either way feel free to enjoy them at the allowed level!). As for chocolate itself, choose dark chocolate. Milk and white chocolates are not considered low-FODMAP due to their lactose content. Do not choose carob products as chocolate alternatives; they contain fructans.

1. Preheat oven to 350°F. Spray six single-cup baking ramekins with coconut oil spray.

2. Purée rice in a food processor. Add avocado, oil, cacao powder, maple syrup, and vanilla; pulse to combine. Scrape down sides of bowl; add eggs and pulse again just until combined.

3. In a separate large bowl, whisk together flour, baking powder, and salt. Drizzle wet ingredients over dry, stirring gently just until combined. Fold in chocolate chips. Do not overmix.

4. Divide batter evenly into ramekins. Bake 18–20 minutes, just until centers are set. Do not overbake.

PER SERVING | Calories: 491 | Fat: 28g | Protein: 7g | Sodium: 335mg | Fiber: 7g | Carbohydrates: 64g | Sugar: 8g

Pumpkin Doughnuts

If you don't have a doughnut pan, you can use this recipe to make mini-muffins.
Divide the batter evenly in a 24-cup mini-muffin pan and increase the bake
time to 18 minutes. Then follow the recipe for dipping in chocolate.

INGREDIENTS | SERVES 12

½ cup canned chickpeas, rinsed

1 cup canned pumpkin

⅓ cup natural peanut butter

1 teaspoon pure vanilla extract

1 tablespoon blackstrap molasses

½ cup pure maple syrup

2 large eggs

½ cup gluten-free oat flour

½ cup almond flour

1 tablespoon pumpkin pie spice

1 teaspoon gluten-free baking powder

¼ teaspoon sea salt

½ cup Dark Chocolate Dip (see recipe in this chapter)

Choose Natural Peanut Butter

Check the label when purchasing peanut butter. Natural peanut butter should have just one ingredient: peanuts. Other peanut butters may contain added fat, sugar, and hydrogenized oils, all of which may be detrimental to your health. You may see that the oil has separated from the solid in the bottle. Give it a good stir and then refrigerate it after opening.

1. Preheat oven to 350°F. Spray a nonstick 24-cup mini-doughnut pan with coconut oil spray.

2. Add chickpeas to a food processor and blend until smooth. Add in pumpkin, peanut butter, vanilla, molasses, maple syrup, and eggs and blend until smooth.

3. In a separate bowl, mix flours, pumpkin pie spice, baking powder, and salt. Add to food processor and pulse just until combined.

4. Divide batter evenly in doughnut pan. Bake 8–10 minutes, or until a toothpick inserted and removed from center of one doughnut side remains clean. Carefully remove donuts and transfer to a cooling rack.

5. Line a baking sheet with parchment paper. Warm the chocolate dip over low heat in a small saucepan. Using a fork or tongs, dip each doughnut into the chocolate to coat all sides. Place on baking sheet.

6. Once all doughnuts are coated, carefully lay sheet flat in freezer for 15 minutes or until chocolate coating is firm and dry to the touch. Transfer to an airtight container for refrigerator storage for up to 3 days.

PER SERVING | Calories: 230 | Fat: 11g | Protein: 8g | Sodium: 151mg | Fiber: 4g | Carbohydrates: 29g | Sugar: 3.5g

Sour Cream Cake

Asked to bring a dessert? This crowd-pleasing make-and-take cake has the look of classic coffee cake, but with an unexpected flavor surprise with the addition of sour cream.

INGREDIENTS | SERVES 9

1 tablespoon lactose-free milk

1 teaspoon white wine vinegar

1 teaspoon cinnamon

1 tablespoon finely ground walnuts

¾ cup plus 1 tablespoon turbinado sugar, divided

2 cups gluten-free oat flour

1 teaspoon gluten-free baking powder

½ teaspoon baking soda

⅛ teaspoon sea salt

3 tablespoons butter, softened

3 tablespoons unrefined coconut oil, softened

1 cup light sour cream

1 teaspoon pure vanilla extract

2 large eggs

1. Preheat oven to 350°F. Line an 8" × 8" baking dish with parchment paper and spray with coconut oil spray.

2. In a small bowl, mix milk and vinegar.

3. In another small bowl, whisk together cinnamon, walnuts, and 1 tablespoon sugar.

4. In a large bowl, whisk together flour, baking powder, baking soda, and salt.

5. In a mixer, cream remaining sugar, butter, and coconut oil. Blend in sour cream, vanilla, and eggs. By hand, stir in milk mixture.

6. Drizzle sour cream mixture over the flour mixture, stirring gently. Do not over-stir. Pour half of batter evenly into baking dish. Sprinkle with half of cinnamon mixture. Pour remaining batter evenly on top; sprinkle with remaining cinnamon mixture.

7. Bake 35 minutes or until a toothpick inserted and removed from center remains clean.

PER SERVING | Calories: 349 | Fat: 20g | Protein: 9g | Sodium: 204mg | Fiber: 3g | Carbohydrates: 34g | Sugar: 1.5g

Ice Cream Sandwiches

This is kid food all grown up! These make-ahead treats add a fun, finishing touch to summer's light dinner fare or a refreshing end to winter's heartiest suppers.

INGREDIENTS | SERVES 4

1½ cups rolled oats

⅛ teaspoon sea salt

1 teaspoon baking soda

1 teaspoon ground cinnamon

½ cup raw cacao powder

½ cup natural peanut butter

1 tablespoon unrefined coconut oil, liquefied

1 cup pure maple syrup

1 pint gluten-free, lactose-free ice cream, softened

Ice Cream and the Low-FODMAP Diet

You may need to do a little investigative work to find ice cream that is gluten- and lactose-free and therefore appropriate for the diet. You may see ingredients, such as carob, inulin, or chicory root, that are not allowed on the diet. As long as their contribution to the product is small (less than 2 percent) you should not have a problem with the product.

1. Preheat oven to 350°F. Line a baking sheet with parchment paper.

2. In a medium bowl, mix together the oats, salt, baking soda, cinnamon, and cacao powder and set aside.

3. In a food processor, blend peanut butter, oil, and maple syrup. Add oat mixture to the peanut butter mixture in the food processor.

4. With moist hands, form rounded tablespoons of the mixture and place on parchment-lined baking sheet (several inches apart, as cookies will spread).

5. Bake 8–10 minutes, or until cookies are fully set. Press very gently on the centers with a spatula; only a light imprint should appear when cookies are done. Cool completely on sheet before transferring.

6. Once cookies are completely cool, place a generous scoop of ice cream on top of each of four cookies. Top each with another cookie and press gently between sheets of waxed paper till sandwiches form.

7. Wrap and freeze sandwiches until ready to serve.

PER SERVING | Calories: 669 | Fat: 28g | Protein: 17g | Sodium: 640mg | Fiber: 9g | Carbohydrates: 100g | Sugar: 19g

Sweet Potato Pudding

This recipe requires a little pre-planning, but is still super-simple. Roast the sweet potatoes one day, then whip up this delicious pudding the next day for an after-dinner dessert.

INGREDIENTS | SERVES 4

2 large sweet potatoes, washed

1 (14.5-ounce) can coconut milk, refrigerated

½ teaspoon pure vanilla extract

1 tablespoon pure maple syrup

¼ teaspoon ground cinnamon

1. Preheat oven to 400°F. Poke a few holes in each sweet potato and place in a small lined baking dish. Roast the sweet potatoes for 50 minutes. Refrigerate overnight.

2. The next day, scoop out the sweet potato flesh and add to a food processor.

3. Open the can of coconut milk and separate the liquid from the solid. Add solid to the food processor, along with the vanilla and maple syrup. (Save liquid from coconut milk for a smoothie or other use.) Blend well.

4. Scoop into pudding cups. Serve immediately, or store in coldest part of refrigerator. Sprinkle with cinnamon just before serving.

PER SERVING | Calories: 182 | Fat: 11g | Protein: 2g | Sodium: 51mg | Fiber: 2g | Carbohydrates: 21g | Sugar: 3g

CHAPTER 15

Snacks

Almost Classic Hummus

Classic hummus, made with garlic, lots of chickpeas, and tahini, is off-limits. But this clever blend of garlic-infused oil, orange bell peppers, pumpkin seeds, and a diet-approved portion of chickpeas mimics the look, taste, and texture.

INGREDIENTS | SERVES 12

1 medium orange bell pepper, seeded and quartered

¼ cup hulled pumpkin seeds

2 tablespoons Garlic-Infused Oil (see recipe in Chapter 9)

1 cup canned chickpeas, rinsed well

3 tablespoons freshly squeezed lemon juice

½ teaspoon ground cumin

½ teaspoon sea salt

Pumpkin Seeds for Health

Pumpkin seeds are also known as pepitas, although sometimes the term "pepitas" is reserved to describe only hulled pumpkin seeds. Pumpkin seeds are allowed on the low-FODMAP diet and should be enjoyed regularly, as they are a good source of protein, potassium, and many minerals, including iron, magnesium, manganese, and zinc.

1. Preheat broiler. Line a baking sheet with foil paper. Place bell pepper pieces on baking sheet and broil for 8–10 minutes, or until tops begin to char. Cool completely, then peel off and discard skins.

2. Add pumpkin seeds and oil to a food processor and blend to a paste consistency.

3. Add pepper pieces, chickpeas, lemon juice, cumin, and salt and blend well.

4. Serve immediately or transfer to an airtight container and store in the refrigerator for up to 1 week.

PER SERVING | Calories: 100 | Fat: 5g | Protein: 4g | Sodium: 103mg | Fiber: 3g | Carbohydrates: 11g | Sugar: 2g

Carrot Dip

Enjoy this dip with brown rice crackers, gluten-free pretzels, or raw low-FODMAP crudité (if tolerable) as a snack for two. Or, if it's just for you, save the leftovers and use as a soup swirl-in, salad dressing, or sandwich spread.

INGREDIENTS | SERVES 2

1 large carrot, peeled and cut into 3" pieces

¼ teaspoon sesame oil

1 teaspoon orange juice

1 teaspoon pure maple syrup

¼ teaspoon pure vanilla extract

¼ teaspoon freshly grated gingerroot

⅛ teaspoon sea salt

Add all ingredients to a high-speed blender or food processor and process to a dip consistency. Add water, 1 tablespoon at a time, to achieve desired thinness.

PER SERVING | Calories: 86 | Fat: 3.5g | Protein: 0.715g | Sodium: 349mg | Fiber: 2g | Carbohydrates: 13g | Sugar: 4g

Minty Melon Mélange

This refreshing blend of herbs and fruit satisfies morning, noon, and night: Serve with lactose-free yogurt in the morning, with strips of sugar-cured ham in the afternoon, or as a standalone, after-dinner treat.

INGREDIENTS | SERVES 4

1 cup diced cantaloupe

1 cup diced honeydew melon

1 tablespoon chopped fresh mint leaves

1 tablespoon torn fresh basil leaves

Toss all ingredients together and serve.

PER SERVING | Calories: 29 | Fat: 0.148g | Protein: 0.625g | Sodium: 14mg | Fiber: 0.798g | Carbohydrates: 7g | Sugar: 6.5g

Citrusy Salsa

Getting in your "five a day" is easy when you pile them all into one delicious salsa! Serve with unsalted, gluten-free tortilla chips. For a sweeter, less tart outcome, simply omit or reduce the lemon and/or lime. Refrigerating this dish for a few hours will enhance its overall flavor.

INGREDIENTS | SERVES 2

1 small lemon, peeled, seeded, and diced

1 small lime, peeled, seeded, and diced

1 small orange, peeled, seeded, and diced

1 small kiwi, peeled and diced

1 cup diced pineapple

½ teaspoon freshly grated gingerroot

1 tablespoon shredded unsweetened coconut

Toss all ingredients in a medium bowl and serve.

PER SERVING | Calories: 237 | Fat: 3g | Protein: 4g | Sodium: 10mg | Fiber: 12g | Carbohydrates: 60g | Sugar: 29g

Rainbow Salsa

Tomatoes come in a variety of shapes and sizes. Experiment with a colorful, flavorful mix of grape, cherry, cocktail, plum, and exotic varieties.

INGREDIENTS | SERVES 4

1 tablespoon extra-virgin olive oil

2 tablespoons diced red onion

1 garlic clove, peeled and slightly crushed

1 cup tomatoes, seeded, cored, and diced

1 tablespoon chopped fresh cilantro

1 tablespoon fresh lime juice

⅛ teaspoon sea salt

½ medium avocado, peeled, pitted, and diced

1. Heat oil in a small skillet over medium heat. Add onion and garlic. Sauté until fragrant. Remove and discard onion and garlic, reserving oil. Set aside to cool.

2. Transfer oil to a medium bowl and toss in tomatoes, cilantro, lime juice, and salt.

3. Stir in avocado just before serving.

PER SERVING | Calories: 72 | Fat: 6g | Protein: 0.894g | Sodium: 79mg | Fiber: 2g | Carbohydrates: 4g | Sugar: 2g

Avocados and the Low-FODMAP Diet

Larger servings of avocado contain levels of polyols that will not be well tolerated. Restrict your serving to ⅛ of a whole avocado and you should be fine. Avocados are a nice source of the "good" fats that help to reduce cholesterol and so are an optimal part of a healthy diet.

Fruit and Cheese Crostini

Experiment with a variety of low-FODMAP fruit, cheese, and herb combinations. These little snacks also make great passed hors d'oeuvres.

INGREDIENTS | SERVES 2

2 slices gluten-free bread, lightly toasted
2 tablespoons frozen cranberries, thawed
1" cube Camembert cheese, quartered
¼ teaspoon dried thyme
½ teaspoon pure maple syrup

1. Preheat broiler. Line a baking sheet with foil.

2. Using a round cookie cutter, cut circles out of each slice of toast.

3. Top each round with 1 tablespoon cranberries, two quarters of cheese, and sprinkle of thyme.

4. Place rounds on lined baking sheet.

5. Broil for 1–2 minutes, or until cheese melts. Drizzle with maple syrup and serve immediately.

PER SERVING | Calories: 100 | Fat: 0.603g | Protein: 4g | Sodium: 209mg | Fiber: 1g | Carbohydrates: 20g | Sugar: 1g

Chocolaty Trail Mix

Store-bought trail mixes are typically filled with dried fruit, which is not allowed on the diet, so it is best to make your own mix.

INGREDIENTS | SERVES 4

1 tablespoon pure maple syrup
1 tablespoon raw cacao powder
⅛ teaspoon sea salt
1 teaspoon butter, melted
1 cup raw peanuts
¼ cup hulled sunflower seeds
¼ cup hulled pumpkin seeds
½ cup dark chocolate chips
½ cup gluten-free pretzel sticks
½ cup potato chips

1. Preheat oven to 350°F. Line two baking sheets with parchment paper.

2. In a small bowl, mix together maple syrup, cacao powder, salt, and butter.

3. In a medium bowl, mix together nuts and seeds.

4. Add maple/cacao mixture to nut mixture and stir to coat. Transfer to one of the baking sheets.

5. Bake for 15 minutes and set aside to cool.

6. Meanwhile, put chocolate chips into a small saucepan and place it over low heat just until chocolate is melted, stirring occasionally. Remove from heat, tilt pan slightly, and dip one end of each pretzel stick in liquid chocolate to coat. Set on remaining baking sheet. When all pretzels have been dipped, transfer sheet to freezer for 5 minutes or until chocolate has hardened.

7. In a large airtight container, combine cooled nut/seed mixture and pretzel sticks. If serving immediately, add potato chips. Otherwise, store mixture in fridge and add potato chips prior to serving.

PER SERVING | Calories: 435 | Fat: 34g | Protein: 15g | Sodium: 88mg | Fiber: 6g | Carbohydrates: 27g | Sugar: 13g

Maple Molasses Trail Mix

Whether you are hiking over mountains or over to the office break room,
this mix offers a take-along antioxidant-filled energy boost.

INGREDIENTS | SERVES 4

1 tablespoon pure maple syrup

½ teaspoon blackstrap molasses

⅛ teaspoon ground allspice

⅛ teaspoon sea salt

1 teaspoon butter, melted

½ cup shelled almonds

½ cup shelled pecans

¼ cup hulled sunflower seeds

¼ cup hulled pumpkin seeds

½ cup gluten-free pretzel sticks

½ cup sweet potato chips

1. Preheat oven to 350°F. Line a baking sheet with parchment paper.

2. In a small bowl, mix together maple syrup, molasses, allspice, salt, and butter.

3. In a medium bowl, mix together nuts and seeds.

4. Add liquid mixture to nut mixture, stir to coat, and transfer to baking sheet. Bake for 10 minutes and set aside to cool.

5. Once completely cool, transfer nuts and seeds to a large bowl, then add in pretzels and sweet potato chips. Gently toss to combine.

6. Store in an airtight container.

PER SERVING | Calories: 410 | Fat: 26g | Protein: 11g | Sodium: 468mg | Fiber: 5g | Carbohydrates: 37.5g | Sugar: 3g

Peppercorn Chicken Wings

These wings are perfect whenever you are looking for a more substantial snack. They also can be whipped up for a crowd as long as you increase marinade ingredients in proportion to the amount of wings you want to serve.

INGREDIENTS | SERVES 4

¼ cup white wine vinegar

1 tablespoon whole peppercorns

2 tablespoons demerara sugar

2 tablespoons Dijon mustard

2 tablespoons gluten-free tamari

1 teaspoon sea salt

3 tablespoons extra-virgin olive oil

2 pounds chicken wing pieces

1. In a blender or food processor, blend vinegar, peppercorns, sugar, mustard, tamari, and salt until peppercorns are chopped. Add olive oil and pulse briefly until incorporated.

2. Place chicken in a large bowl. Pour peppercorn marinade over chicken, tossing to cover completely. Marinate at room temperature for 30 minutes.

3. Preheat oven to 475°F. Line a baking sheet with aluminum foil. Place wings, skin side up, on the lined baking sheet. Brush on extra marinade. Bake for 30 minutes.

4. Change oven to broiler setting. Broil wings for 3 minutes to crisp up. Serve hot or at room temperature.

PER SERVING | Calories: 627 | Fat: 46g | Protein: 42g | Sodium: 1,292mg | Fiber: 0.746g | Carbohydrates: 8g | Sugar: 6.5g

Cranberry Walnut Balls

These raw nut-berry treats are simple to make and so delicious—and with many blended ingredients, easy on the digestive system too. As of this writing, dried cranberries are the only dried fruit allowed in all phases of the diet, as long as you keep your serving size to 1 tablespoon.

INGREDIENTS | SERVES 12

¼ cup maple syrup
¼ cup lactose-free milk
¾ cup chopped walnuts
2 cups gluten-free rolled oats, divided
1 tablespoon plus 1 teaspoon ground cinnamon, divided
½ cup dried cranberries

1. In a small bowl, whisk milk and maple syrup.

2. In a food processor, pulse walnuts to a finely ground flour-like consistency. Transfer one tablespoon of ground walnuts to a plate. Add ½ cup oats and 1 teaspoon cinnamon; mix together. Set aside.

3. Add 1½ cup rolled oats, 1 tablespoon cinnamon, and dried cranberries to the ground walnuts in the food processor. Process until ground to a paste. Add syrup mixture. With moist hands, divide mixture and shape into a dozen balls. Roll each ball in dry oat mixture until coated on all sides.

4. Transfer to an airtight container and firm in refrigerator for at least 2 hours.

PER SERVING | Calories: 137 | Fat: 6g | Protein: 3g | Sodium: 4mg | Fiber: 3g | Carbohydrates: 20g | Sugar: 8g

Broiled Spiced Orange

*This recipe uses ginger, but there are many other variations: cinnamon, nutmeg, or allspice.
Or in lieu of the spices, brush on a drop or two of vanilla or almond extract.*

INGREDIENTS | SERVES 1

1 large orange
½ teaspoon freshly grated gingerroot, divided

1. Preheat broiler. Line a baking sheet with foil.

2. Take a small slice off each end of orange. Slice orange through its middle. Set each orange half on a cutting board, exposed fruit side up. Cut around each orange segment, leaving segments intact. Sprinkle ¼ teaspoon of ginger over each orange half. Place oranges—exposed fruit side up—onto baking sheet.

3. Broil 2–4 minutes, until tops are just starting to brown. Cool for 1–2 minutes and serve warm.

PER SERVING | Calories: 87 | Fat: 0.228g | Protein: 2g | Sodium: 0.13mg | Fiber: 4g | Carbohydrates: 22g | Sugar: 17g

CHAPTER 16

Drinks

Cranberry Festive Water

Eight glasses of water a day can get pretty boring. Pick your happy hour each day to add color and flavor to your water. It will feel like cocktail hour has arrived, but so much healthier without the booze.

INGREDIENTS | SERVES 1

3 freeze-dried cranberries

1 teaspoon lemon zest, freshly grated

1 tablespoon lemon juice

Add all ingredients to an 8-ounce glass of water and serve.

PER SERVING | Calories: 4 | Fat: 0.057g | Protein: 0.11g | Sodium: 3mg | Fiber: 0.185g | Carbohydrates: 1g | Sugar: 0.476g

Water for Optimal Digestion

Drinking plenty of water is essential for digestion. Water helps to keep stool moist and moving! If you don't drink an adequate amount of water, your body will draw water out of the stool, leaving you at risk for constipation. It is best to drink filtered tap or bottled water whenever possible to reduce your exposure to toxins.

Orange Ginger Festive Water

Infuse some pizzazz in your water glass. Add some vitamin C and immune-boosting ginger to your water and drink to your good health!

INGREDIENTS | SERVES 1

2 orange slices

1 teaspoon freshly grated ginger

1 piece candied ginger for garnish

Add all ingredients to an 8-ounce glass of water and serve.

PER SERVING | Calories: 45 | Fat: 0.169g | Protein: 0.642g | Sodium: 5mg | Fiber: 1g | Carbohydrates: 11g | Sugar: 9g

Berry Banana Green Smoothie

Green smoothies are a great way to get more of those super-nutritious greens into your diet. Spinach is a good starter due to its mild taste. As you get more adventurous, feel free to substitute any low-FODMAP green such as kale or Swiss chard.

INGREDIENTS | MAKES 2 CUPS

1 cup rice milk

1 cup packed baby spinach leaves

1 medium firm banana

⅓ cup frozen strawberries

⅓ cup frozen blueberries

⅓ cup frozen raspberries

Combine all ingredients in blender and run until smooth.

PER SERVING (1 CUP) | Calories: 194 | Fat: 3g | Protein: 6g | Sodium: 75mg | Fiber: 6g | Carbohydrates: 40g | Sugar: 26g

Frozen Bananas

You no longer need to throw out bananas that get too ripe, too fast. Simply peel and freeze in an airtight freezer bag, where they will keep for 6–8 months. Frozen bananas make a great base for smoothies.

Peanut Butter Green Smoothie

Next time you are craving sweets, whip up this candy-like smoothie. The presence of kale can help you to justify this decadent treat. Cacao powder offers all of the wonderful phytonutrients of dark chocolate without the sugar.

INGREDIENTS | SERVES 2

2 cups kale (2 leaves)
1 cup rice milk
1 tablespoon raw cacao powder
1 tablespoon natural peanut butter
1 firm medium banana

1. Place kale in blender with rice milk. Blend until smooth. If necessary, pour mixture through strainer, then return to blender.

2. Add all other ingredients to blender and blend until smooth.

PER SERVING | Calories: 205 | Fat: 7g | Protein: 9g | Sodium: 129mg | Fiber: 5g | Carbohydrates: 31g | Sugar: 13g

"Café au Lait"

Craving coffee in the afternoon, but drank your only allowed cup in the morning? Try this for a healthier stand-in. For an indulgent treat, whisk in a tablespoon of Whipped Cream (see recipe in Chapter 14) and sprinkle with ground cinnamon.

INGREDIENTS | SERVES 1

⅓ cup blackstrap molasses

3 teaspoons ground cinnamon

½ cup warmed lactose-free milk

1. In a small bowl, combine the molasses with the cinnamon to form a paste.

2. Whisk 1 teaspoon of paste into ½ cup warmed lactose-free milk.

PER SERVING (1 TEASPOON) | Calories: 15 | Fat: 0.005g | Protein: 0.017g | Sodium: 3mg | Fiber: 0.2g | Carbohydrates: 4g | Sugar: 4g

Golden Changria

Raise your glass with a fresh take on the classic sangria, here featuring the flavors of Chardonnay, vanilla bean, and fresh raspberries. You can experiment with other variations. Try Riesling with sliced low-FODMAP citrus fruits and a sprig of rosemary or Zinfandel with sliced strawberries and a cinnamon stick.

INGREDIENTS | SERVES 8

1 (750-ml) bottle Chardonnay

1 cup Simple Brown Syrup (see recipe in this chapter)

1 whole vanilla bean

2 cups raspberries

2 cups sparkling water

1. In a large pitcher, stir wine and syrup. Drop in vanilla bean and raspberries.

2. Cover and refrigerate overnight.

3. Just before serving, add sparkling water.

PER SERVING | Calories: 247 | Fat: 0.2g | Protein: 1g | Sodium: 9.5mg | Fiber: 3g | Carbohydrates: 33g | Sugar: 25g

Muddled Citrus Sours

You won't miss the maraschino cherries once you taste these subtly spiced cocktails.
If you don't have a muddler, you can use the end of a wooden spoon.

INGREDIENTS | SERVES 4

8 cardamom pods

1 medium orange, peeled and quartered

1 medium lemon, peeled and quartered

1 medium lime, peeled and quartered

1 cup cubed pineapple

½ cup whiskey

½ cup Simple Brown Syrup (see recipe in this chapter)

Filtered water, as needed

1. At the bottom of each of four 8-ounce glasses, place 2 cardamom pods, a quarter each of orange, lemon, and lime, and ¼ cup pineapple. Muddle to release fruit juices and crush the pods.

2. Mix whiskey and syrup in a small pitcher.

3. Top the fruit in each glass with 4 ice cubes, ¼ cup whiskey mixture, and filtered water, leaving enough room to stir, and serve.

PER SERVING | Calories: 306 | Fat: 3g | Protein: 5g | Sodium: 37mg | Fiber: 14g | Carbohydrates: 75g | Sugar: 8g

Rosy Vodkatini

Flavor this festive cocktail seasonally—with mint leaves in spring, basil leaves in summer, rosemary or thyme sprigs in fall, and a cinnamon stick in winter.

INGREDIENTS | SERVES 4

½ cup dried cranberries
1 sprig of rosemary
1 cup boiling water
1 cup cranberry juice
8 ounces vodka

1. Soak cranberries and rosemary in 1 cup boiling water for at least 2 hours.

2. Using a fine mesh sieve, drain the cranberry mixture, reserving the liquid and discarding the fruit and herb.

3. For each drink, pour 2 ounces each of cranberry/herb water, cranberry juice, and vodka into a cocktail shaker filled with ice. Cover and shake. Strain into a chilled martini glass and serve.

PER SERVING | Calories: 206 | Fat: 0.4g | Protein: 0.3g | Sodium: 4mg | Fiber: 1g | Carbohydrates: 20g | Sugar: 18g

Maple Walnut Cups

These pretty teacups can be prepared up to a day ahead and refrigerated. Served with warm rice milk—or coffee or tea—they're an easy way to wow your after-dinner guests or treat yourself to a special dessert beverage any time.

INGREDIENTS | SERVES 4

4 cups plus ¼ cup rice milk

⅛ teaspoon arrowroot powder

1 tablespoon raw sugar

1 teaspoon maple sugar, divided

1 tablespoon finely ground shelled walnuts

1 drop pure vanilla extract

Relaxation and a Warm Toddy

You are only allowed one cup of coffee per day on the low-FODMAP diet, so save that for the morning. In lieu of that after-dinner cup of coffee, put a relaxed body to bed by treating yourself to a warm, caffeine-free drink in the evening.

1. In a small bowl, mix ¼ cup rice milk with arrowroot. Transfer to the center of a small plate and allow to thicken for at least 5 minutes.

2. On a separate small plate, mix raw sugar and ½ teaspoon maple sugar with walnuts.

3. Line up four teacups. Dip each teacup's rim into the milk mixture to coat, then into the walnut mixture. Set teacups aside to set for at least 5 minutes.

4. In a small saucepan, warm remaining rice milk. Add remaining maple sugar and vanilla extract and stir.

5. Avoiding the rims, pour warm milk in even amounts into each teacup and serve.

PER SERVING | Calories: 167 | Fat: 6g | Protein: 9g | Sodium: 132mg | Fiber: 2g | Carbohydrates: 20g | Sugar: 14g

Pumpkin Cinnamon Cups

While impressive for entertaining, the use of these pretty teacups can really brighten up an ordinary day or weeknight. Cups can be prepared and stored in the refrigerator up to a day ahead. Sip this soothing drink in the evenings to relax after a busy day.

INGREDIENTS | SERVES 4

¼ cup canned pumpkin

4 cups plus ¼ cup rice milk, divided

1 tablespoon raw sugar

1 tablespoon ground cinnamon

IBS and Sleep

Research has shown that IBS symptoms can be worse in the morning following a bad night's sleep. You can help to ensure a good night's sleep if you avoid heavy meals, excess sugar, alcohol, and caffeine for at least three hours before going to bed.

1. In a small bowl, mix pumpkin and ¼ cup rice milk. Transfer to the center of a small plate.

2. On a separate small plate, mix raw sugar and cinnamon.

3. Line up four teacups. Dip each teacup's rim into the pumpkin mixture to coat, then into the cinnamon mixture to coat. Set teacups aside to set for at least 5 minutes.

4. In a small saucepan, warm remaining rice milk.

5. Avoiding the rims, pour warm milk in even amounts into each teacup and serve.

PER SERVING | Calories: 161 | Fat: 4.5g | Protein: 9g | Sodium: 133mg | Fiber: 3g | Carbohydrates: 22g | Sugar: 14g

Simple Brown Syrup

You can experiment with the thickness and flavor of this sweet liquid beverage base by varying the sugar-to-water ratio. Using demerara or muscovado sugar will intensify the flavor.

INGREDIENTS | MAKES 1½ CUPS

1 cup turbinado sugar
1 cup filtered water

Heat sugar and water in a saucepan over low heat, stirring often, just until crystals dissolve. Remove from heat and bring to room temperature or cool before using.

PER SERVING (1 TEASPOON) | Calories: 28 | Fat: 0g | Protein: 0g | Sodium: 1mg | Fiber: 0g | Carbohydrates: 5g | Sugar: 4g

Appendix A

Sample Menu Plan

Although you will want to be doing more home cooking as you follow the low-FODMAP diet, you need not spend all of your time in the kitchen! With a little planning, you can prepare staple dishes that will be on hand for when you need them. You don't need to save all of your food prep for the weekends—rather, you can prepare one of your must-have items as you cook a weeknight meal.

Breakfast

Unless you are one of those rare people who have all the time in the world in the mornings, you will want some quick and easy options. One idea is to make up a batch of Crunchy Granola—enjoy half now and freeze the other half for next week. Amaranth Breakfast and Quinoa "Carrot Cake" Breakfast can also be prepared ahead for a quick reheat. (See recipes in Chapter 6.)

Lunch

Eating a healthy low-FODMAP lunch is easy if you always have a homemade salad dressing, such as Basic Salad Dressing (see recipe in Chapter 13) or Maple Mustard Salad Dressing, on hand, as well as packaged spinach or arugula. When you have a quick moment you can prepare your tuna and veggies for either the Niçoise Wraps or Tuna Melt "Nachos." Similarly, it will only take a few minutes to prepare your lentils and red pepper for your Lentil Salad over Arugula or put together your Peanutty Noodle Bowl. (See recipes in Chapter 7).

Snacks

When you come home from the market with some fresh low-FODMAP fruit, make up a batch of Minty Melon Mélange to have alongside some lactose-free yogurt for a feel-good snack or healthy dessert. Similarly, make it a point to either have some Citrusy Salsa or Carrot Dip on hand to pair with some gluten-free tortilla chips. Try to keep a bowl of Almost Classic Hummus in the refrigerator, alongside some baby carrots, for an easy midmorning or afternoon snack. In addition, make sure to always keep FODMAP-friendly nuts and seeds around for easy-to-take-anywhere snacks. (See recipes in Chapter 15.)

Dinner

Dinner prep can be a little more time-consuming. Try to make your efforts do double duty and squeeze out a second use for each dish. You could cook an Autumn's Roast Chicken (see recipe in Chapter 11) on the weekend and then enjoy the leftover chicken on your lunch salads. A big pot of soup, such as

Turkey and Brown Rice Soup (see recipe in Chapter 8), makes for a warming supper that can then be enjoyed later in the week for lunch or a midafternoon snack. Leftover Feta Crab Cakes (see recipe in Chapter 12) can make for a next-day lunch that will be the envy of your coworkers.

SAMPLE MENU PLAN

	Day One	Day Two	Day Three	Day Four	Day Five
Breakfast	Crunchy Granola*	Dressed-Up Eggs	Pumpkin Pancakes	Berry Banana Green Smoothie	Cuppa Coffee Cake* with a cup of coffee
Snack	Berry Banana Green Smoothie	Cranberry Walnut Balls* with Cranberry Festive Water	Citrusy Salsa and plain lactose-free yogurt*	Fruit and Cheese Crostini	Almost Classic Hummus* with baby carrots
Lunch	Peanutty Noodle Bowl*	Lentil Salad over Arugula	Bean-Free Minestrone*	Turkey Cranberry Panini	Peanut Butter and "Jam" Sandwich
Snack	Almost Classic Hummus* with brown rice cracker	Fruit and Cheese Crostini	"Café au Lait" with Cuppa Coffee Cake*	Cranberry Walnut Ball	Citrusy Salsa and plain lactose-free yogurt*
Dinner	Bean-Free Minestrone*	Autumn's Roast Chicken with Autumn's Glaze and String Beans and Sweet Potato Fries	Italian Vegetable Sauce* with gluten-free pasta	Turkey Cutlets with Grapes with Toasted Coconut Almond Millet	Smoky Sourdough Pizza

*Can be prepared ahead.

Inspiration and Updates

For more menu planning ideas, recipes, and photos, as well as updates on allowed and restricted foods, please visit *www.EverythingLowFODMAP.com*.

Appendix B

Sources

Barrett, J.S. (2013). Extending our knowledge of fermentable, short-chain carbohydrates for managing gastrointestinal symptoms. *Nutrition in Clinical Practice, 28*, 300–306.

Barrett, J.S., & Gibson, P.R. (2012). Fermentable oligosaccharides, disaccharides, monosaccharides and polyols (FODMAPs) and nonallergic food intolerance: FODMAPs or food chemicals? *Therapeutic Advances in Gastroenterology, 5*, 261–268.

Catsos, P. (2012). *IBS—Free at Last!: Change Your Carbs, Change Your Life* (2nd ed.). Portland, ME: Pond Cove Press.

CEMA, Monash University (2014). The Monash University Low FODMAP Diet (3rd ed.) [Mobile application software]. Retrieved from *www.apple.com/itunes*

Gibson, P.R., & Shepherd, S.J. (2010). Evidence-based dietary management of functional gastrointestinal symptoms: The FODMAP approach. *Journal of Gastroenterology and Hepatology, 25,* 252–258.

Muir, J.G., & Gibson, P.R. (2013). The low FODMAP diet for treatment of irritable bowel syndrome and other gastrointestinal disorders. *Gastroenterology & Hepatology, 9,* 450–452.

Mullin, G.E., & Swift, K.M. (2011). *The Inside Tract: Your Good Gut Guide to Great Digestive Health.* New York: Rodale.

Pimentel, M. (2006). *A New IBS Solution: Bacteria—the Missing Link in Treating Irritable Bowel Syndrome.* Sherman Oaks, CA: Health Point Press.

Shepherd, S., & Gibson, P. (2013). *The Complete Low-FODMAP Diet: A Revolutionary Plan for Managing IBS and Other Digestive Disorders.* New York: The Experiment.

Appendix C

Additional Resources

Everything Low-FODMAP.com
www.everythinglowfodmap.com

Dr. Barbara Bolen
www.drbarbarabolen.com

Kathleen Bradley, CPC
www.kathleenbradley.net

IBS at About.com
www.ibs.about.com

Patsy Catsos, MS, RD, LD: IBS—Free at Last!
www.ibsfree.net

Kate Scarlata, RD, LDN: FODMAPs Checklist
www.blog.katescarlata.com/fodmaps-basics/fodmaps-checklist

The Monash University Low FODMAP Diet Mobile App
https://itunes.apple.com/us/app/monash-university-low-fodmap/id586149216

Monash University Low FODMAP Diet for Irritable Bowel Syndrome
www.med.monash.edu/cecs/gastro/fodmap

Irritable Bowel Syndrome Self Help and Support Group
www.ibsgroup.org

International Foundation for Functional Gastrointestinal Disorders
www.iffgd.org

National Foundation for Celiac Awareness
www.celiaccentral.org

Standard U.S./Metric Measurement Conversions

VOLUME CONVERSIONS

U.S. Volume Measure	Metric Equivalent
⅛ teaspoon	0.5 milliliter
¼ teaspoon	1 milliliter
½ teaspoon	2 milliliters
1 teaspoon	5 milliliters
½ tablespoon	7 milliliters
1 tablespoon (3 teaspoons)	15 milliliters
2 tablespoons (1 fluid ounce)	30 milliliters
¼ cup (4 tablespoons)	60 milliliters
⅓ cup	90 milliliters
½ cup (4 fluid ounces)	125 milliliters
⅔ cup	160 milliliters
¾ cup (6 fluid ounces)	180 milliliters
1 cup (16 tablespoons)	250 milliliters
1 pint (2 cups)	500 milliliters
1 quart (4 cups)	1 liter (about)

WEIGHT CONVERSIONS

U.S. Weight Measure	Metric Equivalent
½ ounce	15 grams
1 ounce	30 grams
2 ounces	60 grams
3 ounces	85 grams
¼ pound (4 ounces)	115 grams
½ pound (8 ounces)	225 grams
¾ pound (12 ounces)	340 grams
1 pound (16 ounces)	454 grams

OVEN TEMPERATURE CONVERSIONS

Degrees Fahrenheit	Degrees Celsius
200 degrees F	95 degrees C
250 degrees F	120 degrees C
275 degrees F	135 degrees C
300 degrees F	150 degrees C
325 degrees F	160 degrees C
350 degrees F	180 degrees C
375 degrees F	190 degrees C
400 degrees F	205 degrees C
425 degrees F	220 degrees C
450 degrees F	230 degrees C

BAKING PAN SIZES

U.S.	Metric
8 × 1½ inch round baking pan	20 × 4 cm cake tin
9 × 1½ inch round baking pan	23 × 3.5 cm cake tin
11 × 7 × 1½ inch baking pan	28 × 18 × 4 cm baking tin
13 × 9 × 2 inch baking pan	30 × 20 × 5 cm baking tin
2 quart rectangular baking dish	30 × 20 × 3 cm baking tin
15 × 10 × 2 inch baking pan	30 × 25 × 2 cm baking tin (Swiss roll tin)
9 inch pie plate	22 × 4 or 23 × 4 cm pie plate
7 or 8 inch springform pan	18 or 20 cm springform or loose-bottom cake tin
9 × 5 × 3 inch loaf pan	23 × 13 × 7 cm or 2 lb narrow loaf or pâté tin
1½ quart casserole	1.5 liter casserole
2 quart casserole	2 liter casserole

Index